THE A-Z OF
QUANTUM
LEAP

OTHER QUANTUM LEAP TITLES
PUBLISHED BY BOXTREE

THE A-Z OF QUANTUM LEAP

by
JULIE BARRETT

Based on the Universal Television series
QUANTUM LEAP
Created by Donald P. Bellisario

B□XTREE

The A-Z of Quantum Leap, a book by Julie Barrett, based on the Universal television series QUANTUM LEAP created by Donald P. Bellisario

First published in the UK 1995 by Boxtree Limited
Broadwall House, 21 Broadwall, London SE1 9PL

10 9 8 7 6 5 4 3 2 1

ISBN: 0 7522 0628 1

Cover art by Colin Howard

Phototypeset by SX Composing Ltd, Rayleigh, Essex
Printed and bound in Great Britain by Cox and Wyman

A CIP catalogue record for this book is available from the British Library

Contents

Introduction

The seed for this book was planted three years ago when I was editing a *Quantum Leap* fanzine called *A Matter of Time*. As I wrote my own stories and edited those of others, I came to realize that my knowledge of the details of the show was somewhat less than encyclopaedic – this despite having watched every episode several times. In all honesty, it's more important for me to keep track of the date the mortgage payment is due than the leap date of any given episode.

One day, in an attempt to avoid having to spend hours running through videotapes for a correct quotation or name, I began a database. My quest was to capture some sort of note on every significant detail, to make my own series bible of sorts. Nearly every item is cross-referenced to the episode in which it was found.

An alphabetical listing of the episode titles precedes the concordance, and after each title is a keyword identifier. I tried to choose unique words from titles, rather than to use ones which might confuse. For example, *Catch a Falling Star* is listed as "CATCH" and *Star Light, Star Bright* is given the keyword "BRIGHT". Some entries or parts of entries do not have a keyword. I have done this for items that are "common knowledge" in the context of the show. Following the concordance is an episode guide with a brief summary of each storyline. Also, the name of each person

Sam has leaped into, with the exception of himself and Al, is listed in boldface for easy reference.

This book is not intended to be an episode guide, as that has been done thoroughly elsewhere. My intention is to provide a reference to the names, places, objects, etc. found in the series. With that in mind, I spent hours exhaustively concurring each episode. Some may think I have gone too far, others may think I could have added more detail. I hope I have managed to find a happy medium (and that's not Alvira, the psychic from *Leaping in Without a Net!*). I have also rechecked many of the items with fans of the series. By this point, any omissions or glaring errors are my own.

It should be noted that some spellings are different in different scripts. For example, the programmer's name has been spelled "Gooshie" and "Gushie", and Verbena Beeks and Albert Calavicci's names have seen several permutations. In this case, I have gone with the screen and TV listing credits used most often. You may notice last names that were never mentioned on the air. These were culled from scripts. For those names and places that were either not mentioned in a script or were used in scripts I had no access to, I used what I considered to be the best spelling.

I would like to gratefully acknowledge the following people, for without them this book would never have been seen beyond the phosphor of my computer monitor: Christina Mavroudis, founder of *Quantum Quarterly* for her initial push in the right direction; Project Quantum Leap founder and president 'Karen Funk Blocher' for her encouragement and help on the details; Terri Bridge, Ann Raymont and Jackie Vansuch for proofreading: and the entire Prodigy Leaper gang for their help and encouragements.

Most of all I would like to thank my husband Paul and son Christopher for their patience and understanding while I completed this project.

I would like to dedicate this book to my father, David West. Like Sam Beckett, I wish I could put right what illness made wrong.

ALPHABETICAL INDEX OF EPISODES

8½ Months, November 15, 1955 (8½),
All-Americans, November 6, 1962 (ALL)
The Americanization of Machiko, August 4, 1953 (MACHIKO)
Animal Frat, October 19, 1967 (FRAT)
Another Mother, September 30, 1981 (MOTHER)
The Beast Within, November 6, 1972 (BEAST)
Black and White on Fire, August 11, 1965 (B&W)
Blind Faith, February 6, 1964 (BLIND)
Blood Moon, March 10, 1965 (BLOOD)
The Boogieman, October 31, 1964 (BMAN)
The Camikazi Kid, June 6, 1961 (CAM)
Catch a Falling Star, May 21, 1979 (CATCH)
The Color of Truth, August 8, 1955 (COLOR)
The Curse of Pta-Hotep, March 2, 1957 (CURSE)
Deliver us From Evil, March 19, 1966 (EVIL)
Disco Inferno, April 1, 1976 (DISCO)
Dreams, February 29, 1979 (DREAMS)
Dr. Ruth, April 25, 1985 (RUTH)
Double Identity, November 8, 1965 (DOUBLE)
Evil Leaper II: Return, October 8, 1956 (RETURN)
Evil Leaper II: Revenge, September 16, 1987 (REVENGE)
For Your Love, June 14, 1966 (TRILOGY)
Freedom, November 22, 1970 (FREEDOM)
Future Boy, October 6, 1957 (FUTURE)
Ghost Ship, August 13, 1951 (SHIP)
Glitter Rock, April 12, 1974 (ROCK)
Good Morning, Peoria, September 9, 1959 (PEORIA)
Good Night, Dear Heart, November 9, 1957 (DEAR)

3

Goodbye, Norma Kean, April 4, 1960 (NORMA)
The Great Spontini, May 9, 1974 (SPONT)
Heart of a Champion, July 23, 1965 (CHAMP)
Her Charm, September 6, 1973 (CHARM)
Honeymoon Express, April 27, 1960 (HONEYMOON)
How the Tess Was Won, August 5, 1956 (TESS)
A Hunting We Will Go, June 18, 1976 (HUNT)
Hurricane, August 17, 1969 (HURRICANE)
It's a Wonderful Leap, May 10, 1958 (WONDERFUL)
Jimmy, October 14, 1964 (JIMMY)
Justice, May 11, 1955 (JUSTICE)
Killin' Time, June 18, 1958 (KILLIN)
Last Dance Before an Execution, May 12, 1971 (LAST)
The Last Door, July 18, 1978 (TRILOGY)
The Last Gunfighter, November 28, 1957 (GUN)
The Leap Back, June 15, 1945; September 18, 1999
   (BACK)
The Leap Between the States, September 20, 1862
   (STATES)
A Leap for Lisa, June 25, 1957 (LISA)
The Leap Home, November 25, 1969 (HOME)
The Leap Home, Pt. II: Vietnam, April 7, 1970 (NAM)
Leap of Faith, August 19, 1963 (FAITH)
Leaping in Without a Net, November 18, 1958 (NET)
Leaping of the Shrew, September 27, 1956 (SHREW)
Lee Harvey Oswald, March 21, 1963; October 5-6, 1957;
   June 6, 1959; October 21, 1959; April 10, 1963;
   October 21, 1963; November 22, 1963 (LHO)
Liberation, October 16, 1968 (LIBERATION)
A Little Miracle, December 24, 1962 (MIRACLE)
M.I.A., April 1, 1969 (MIA)
Maybe Baby, March 11, 1963 (MAYBE)
Memphis Melody, July 3, 1954 (MEMPHIS)
Mirror Image, August 8, 1953 (MIRROR)
Miss Deep South, June 7, 1958 (SOUTH)
Moments to Live, May 4, 1985 (MOMENTS)

4

Nowhere to Run, August 10, 1968 (NOWHERE)
Nuclear Family, October 26, 1962 (NUCLEAR)
One Little Heart, August 8, 1955 (TRILOGY)
One Strobe Over the Line, June 15, 1965 (STROBE)
Permanent Wave, June 2, 1983 (PERM)
Piano Man, November 10, 1985 (PIANO)
Play Ball, August 6, 1961 (BALL)
Play it Again, Seymour, April 14, 1953 (SEYMOUR)
The Play's the Thing, September 9, 1969 (PLAY)
Pool Hall Blues, September 4, 1954 (POOL)
A Portrait for Troian, February 7, 1971 (TROIAN)
Promised Land, December 22, 1971 (LAND)
Private Dancer, October 6, 1979 (DANCER)
Quantum Leap, September 13, 1956; September, 1968
   (PILOT)
Raped, June 20, 1980 (RAPED)
Rebel Without a Clue, September 1, 1958 (REBEL)
The Right Hand of God, October 24, 1974 (RIGHT)
Roberto!, July 27, 1982 (ROBERTO)
Runaway, July 4, 1964 (RUNAWAY)
Running for Honor, June 11, 1964 (HONOR)
Sea Bride, June 3, 1954 (BRIDE)
Shock Theatre, October 3, 1954 (SHOCK)
A Single Drop of Rain, September 7, 1953 (RAIN)
So Help Me God, July 29, 1957 (HELP)
A Song for the Soul, April 7, 1963 (SONG)
Southern Comforts, August 4, 1961 (COMFORTS)
Star Crossed, June 15, 1972 (CROSSED)
Star Light, Star Bright, May 21, 1966 (BRIGHT)
Stand Up, April 30, 1959 (STAND)
A Tale of Two Sweeties, February 25, 1958 (TALE)
Temptation Eyes, February 1, 1985 (EYES)
Thou Shalt Not, February 2, 1974 (SHALT)
Unchained, November 2, 1956 (UNCHAINED)
What Price Gloria?, October 16, 1961 (GLORIA)
The Wrong Stuff, January 24, 1961 (WRONG)

A

ABC Rap

Al made up the words to a rap tune Sam had once programmed into Ziggy's memory banks in order to teach the alphabet to Tibby Johnson, a patient at Havenwell. (SHOCK)

Accelerator Chamber

When Sam first leaped, he was inside a nuclear accelerator chamber located at Project Quantum Leap.

Action Eyes

KSFW-TV's newscast. Their reporter Dylan Powell had been tipped off in advance of each of a string of serial murders. (EYES)

Adams, Henry

Vietnam vet who is living a "mountain man" existence in Washington State in 1972 with his army buddy Roy Brown. Henry had been keeping an eloquent journal that described his days in combat, including the night one of his friends was killed. Henry, Roy, Luke Marlet and John Burke were high school buddies who signed up after graduation and served together with John leading the group. Luke had disobeyed a direct order to kill an old man inside a hooch (bar), and when John went in to do the job, the hooch exploded, killing John. (BEAST)

Adams Hotel

Gina Dorleac was last seen at this New Orleans hotel before she vanished. (COMFORTS)

Addison Men's Club

Activist Diana St. Cloud staged a walkout at this men-only establishment, which hasn't had a woman in the dining room in 200 years. (LIBERATION)

Aggie

The beautician in Raven Roc, MA. She "made up" the bodies for the mortician, and also performed abortions on the side. She had been asked to perform an abortion on Hilla Danner, but Hilla couldn't go through with it. Ziggy says that later, in 1963, she was indicated for performing illegal abortions, but was never convicted. (DEAR)

Also the name of a milk cow on the Beckett farm. (HOME)

Aider, Bart

Abagail Fuller was the last person to see him alive. When Sam leaped in, he found Bart dead of what appeared to be a blow to the head, but the local doctor pronounced it to have been a heart attack. The question was: Did the blow happen before or after? (TRILOGY)

Aider, Leta

She lost her daughter in 1953, and her husband two years later, and believed Abagail Fuller was responsible for both deaths. Eleven years later, she led a lynch mob that tried to kill Abagail after a local boy went missing. The boy was eventually found safe. In 1978, her daughter's bones were found at the bottom of a well. Leta went to an attorney, but he told her that they couldn't prosecute Abagail because she was a juvenile when the murder took place. Leta was later found in Abagail's kitchen, dead, and Abagail was arrested for the murder. At the trial it came out that Leta had committed suicide, but called the Sheriff just before killing herself to report screams in the house so as to set up Abagail. (TRILOGY)

Aider, Violet

Next to Abagail Fuller, she was the prettiest girl in the parish in 1953, but she vanished after the two girls had an argument over a locket. The entire parish searched for her until they found her bloody sweater and decided a pack of wild dogs roaming in the area must have killed her. They destroyed the dogs and sheriff Clayton Fuller closed the case. Her bones were discovered in 1978 when the town well was unsealed for renovations. (TRILOGY)

Al the Bartender

Proprietor of Al's Place, a bar in Cokeburg, PA. His full name is Alberto. Philosophical and enigmatic, Al dispenses advice along with the drinks. Everything about Al's Place is strange to Sam. First, nearly everyone in the bar either looks like someone he's known on a previous leap, or shares a name with a close friend of his – or both. Sam slowly comes to the conclusions that Al is actually God or Time or whoever is leaping him around. Al denies it and insists that Sam is the agent of his own destiny. (MIRROR)

Al's Place

A bar in the mining town of Cokeburg, PA. Sam walked in at 12:30 p.m. on August 8, 1953 – the exact moment he was born. From there, things got even more strange. Nearly everyone who visited the bar appeared to Sam to be someone have had seen on a previous leap. One miner looked like Moe Stein. Another pair looked like Jimmy and Frank LaMotta. Not only was there the odd co-incidence of the bartender being named after Sam's best friend, but two other people were also named Ziggy and Gooshie, and Gooshie had bad breath. When Sam looked at these people in the mirror, instead of the reflections he expected he saw different people wearing the same cloth-ing. (MIRROR)

Alberta

The pool cue belonging to Charlie "Black Magic" Walters is as big a legend as he is. Named after his wife, it's 21 ounces of pure African ebony inlaid with mother-of-pearl. (POOL)

Ali, Muhammad

He and George Foreman fought it out for the World Heavyweight boxing title on October 29, 1974. Sam was able to place a bet on the fight and solve a lot of Kid Cody's problems with the winnings. (HAND)

Alia

If Sam was able to travel in time, it stands to reason that some time another person would do the same. Perhaps it was a greater shock than a surprise when Sam encountered Alia. When they first met, Sam had leaped back into Jimmy LaMotta's life, and Alia had become Connie. They didn't find out about each other until they touched, which set up a magnetic convergence field allowing them to see each other. Alia told Sam that she was with a time travel experiment, and she too suffered from swiss-cheese memory and had no control over where she was going to go. But the one thing she really wanted was to go home. She then tried to seduce Sam, saying that he was the only one who could understand what she was going through. Their lovemaking was interrupted by Frank's early return. While Sam was digging for his clothes, Alia ripped her slip, scratched her face, and screamed that Jimmy had tried to rape her. Zoey, her observer, then reported that she had to kill Sam, and that doing it could get her home. Alia explained to Sam it wasn't God that set them against each other. Sam countered by postulating that evil could only exist because of good, and if she killed him she might no longer exist, and it would only add to the power of whatever was leaping her around. Alia has apparently killed a lot of people, but she was unable to bring herself to kill Sam, and Alia and Zoey exited, distorted and screaming in pain.

When the pair met again, Alia told Sam that she had been tortured, and that the experience was worse than death. She begged Sam not to let her go through that kind of pain again, so Sam suggested that if they were to hold each other when they leaped, they might be able to go together. They did, right into Mallard Correctional Facility for Women. In an attempt to keep Lothos from locking on to her brainwaves, Sam altered them slightly by hypnotizing her into believing she actually was the woman into whom she had leaped.

While Alia doesn't seem to be completely evil (otherwise why would she want to be redeemed?), she does wonder why some people help other people. Obviously such behaviour is either not in her background or has been conditioned out by some means.

Alia could see Zoey's observer, Thames.

When Alia was shot by Zoey, she leaped out and Angel Jenson leaped back in. Angel was unhurt. Lothos reported that Alia was lost, and Ziggy reported to Al that she was free. (EVIL, RETURN, REVENGE)

'All I Have to do is Dream'

On the soap opera *Moments to Live*, Dr. Craig Hall had played this Everly Brothers tune the night he and Rebecca Wainscroft had a midnight dinner on the roof of his penthouse apartment. After Norma Kean Pilcher kidnapped the actor who played Hall, she used it in an attempt to seduce him/Sam. (MOMENTS)

Allen, Nick

Sam leaped into this detective who could double for Bogart while holding a gun over the body of Allen's dead partner Phil Grimsley. He was there to solve the murder, but kept having a feeling of *déjà vu*. All was explained when he found a manuscript in Nick's desk. Sam realized it was a book he had once read. The working title was *Dead Men Don't Die*, but it was published under the title of *Who Killed Grimsley and Allen?*, a mystery the readers were invited to solve. No one did. (SEYMOUR)

Allen, Woody

When he saw Nick Allen at LaGuardia Airport, he mistook the detective for Bogart, and immediately launched into a spiel about his girlfriend Annie and how his mother made him neurotic. (SEYMOUR)

Alpha

One of the changes made when Sam briefly altered Al's history in 1957 was that Ziggy had been named Alpha. (LISA)

Alvira

One of the "harem girls" (strippers) at the circus where Sam worked as Victor Panzini. She and Victor apparently had a thing going. (NET)

American Sign Language (ASL)

Sam tried to learn ASL in order to communicate better with Diana Quina, a deaf dancer he was helping out. One of the things he learned was ASL for Quantum Leap. (DANCER)

Anderson, Rudolph Jr., Major

U-2 pilot shot down over Cuba in 1962. Al flew over Cuba afterwards. (NUCLEAR)

Angela, Sister

One of a group of nuns who had inherited the contract for boxer Kid Cody. Angela was determined to build a grand chapel and street mission in Sacramento. When she was a child she was the only survivor of a house fire. She grew up being shuffled between her uncles, and finally ran away and ended up on the streets. After the stumbled into a skid row chapel, a nun helped her restore her faith in herself and in God. Angela then decided to dedicate her life to helping others and to build a chapel toward that purpose. (HAND)

Anita

An actress in the touring company performing *The Man of La Mancha* who was seeing John O'Malley, the star of the troupe. (CATCH)

Arden, Dr.

In charge of the centrifuge at Cape Canaveral in 1961 (WRONG)

Arnett, Jackie

This pretty girl lived near Kevin Bruckner and attended the same school and had a reputation for being fast. Rumor was that the whole track team had had her. She reluctantly agreed to set Kevin up for his "initiation" as a Wizard, and in return she would get to go to Mardi Gras with the class president and be crowned queen. (MOTHER)

Ashcroft, Phillip

Kicked out of Prescott Naval Academy because he was gay, he attempted to retaliate by printing up a list containing what he believed to be the name of every gay cadet at the academy. Sam and the track coach talked him out of suicide, and he eventually went to Greenwich Village and worked at the Stonewall Bar. The bar would later be the scene of a riot that was widely believed to be a turning point in the Gay Rights movement. (HONOR)

Ashton, Leslie, Dr.

Top vet on Project Mercury at age 27. She got her Veterinary degree in London from the Royal veterinary College and a Ph.D. in Animal Behavior from London University, but grew up in Cameroon, where they made the wrappers for Al's Chivello cigars. Her father was a surgeon, and he packed the family off to West Africa when she was there. He gave up a good London practice to help unfortunate people. She ended up starting her own veterinary practice in Santa Fe in 1965, and eventually built a sanctuary for orphaned and ex-research chimps. (WRONG)

Atuna, Julio

He had been a doctor in Cuba, but was unable to obtain his medical license in the States, so he swept floors in a pharmacy, stealing medicine for needy people. He was with Raul Casta when Casta was alleged to have murdered Father Torelli, but never showed up for the trial. District Attorney Theodore Moody had offered him a chance to get his license in New York if he left the state and wouldn't testify. (LAST)

B

B-50

The "Mother Hen" which transported the X-2 test plane to is flying altitude. (PILOT)

BB

A militant friend of the Harper Brothers, he dragged Lonnie and Poppa Dee out looting and rioting after the Watts riots began. (B&W)

Barko Bites

"Shaped like tiny little cats for the treats dogs love to eat." (BLIND)

Barrenger, Dana

This 32-year-old woman was once the personal secretary of the notorious Nick Kochifas. She found out about Nick's shady deals, and went to the Justice Department. Although she testified against him at his trial, Nick was acquitted, probably because he bought off the judge and/or jury. He vowed revenge on Dana, so she was placed in the witness protection progam. Her murder was originally set up by FBI agent Peter Langly, the man assigned to protect her. After Sam took her to Professor LoNigro's Berkshires cabin, she married LoNigro and became a lawyer. (CHARM)

Barry, Delilah (Lila)

Sam found himself defending this black woman on charges of murdering the son of her white employer.

After Sam proved her innocence, she left town to start a new life. Sam met her at the bus stop and gave her a primer, telling her she would be truly free if she learned how to read. (HELP)

Bartlett

The only member of the Committee whose wife Al would sleep with. (CROSSED)

Basch, Danny

He died in 1973, and his father was so upset that a year later he still hadn't set the stone on the grave. He and a friend named Mark had gone backpacking alone in Europe and died in a plane crash. (SHALT)

Basch, David

Oy, veh! He's the rabbi! Sam's task was to prevent David's sister-in-law Irene from having a one-night stand and ruining her marriage. (SHALT)

Basch, Irene

She blamed herself for the death of her son Danny because she talked her husband Joe into letting him go to Europe. Her husband seemed to blame her too, which was putting a strain on the entire family. (SHALT)

Basch, Joe

Irene's husband was having a hard time adjusting to the death of his son a year before, and his relationship with his wife and daughter had deteriorated to the point that the family was on the brink of collapse. After Sam reunited them, he and Irene wrote a book on dealing with the loss of a family member. (SHALT)

Basch, Karen

Sam leaped into her Bar Mitzvah ceremony on February 2, 1974. (SHALT)

Bathory, Count

According to the legend that was recounted to Sam, Count Bathory was one of the first vampires in recorded history, and was personally responsible for the ritual deaths of 650 virgins. He believed that their blood would give him eternal life. The townspeople caught him and walled him up inside his bedroom where he stayed alive for three years drinking his own blood. They say the night he left his confinement the moon turned blood red, and ever since then it's been required to offer up a sacrifice in his name. Legend has it that Bathory himself had been at that castle 300 years before. In reality, there was a Countess Erszabet

Bathory, who was reputed to have committed many of the acts ascribed to the fictional count. (BLOOD)

Battling Rooskies

The wrestling world knew them as Ivan and Nikoli, two fierce Muscovites who together weighed 510 pounds. Behind the accents and red hammer and sickle-emblazoned tights were Ronnie and Terry Sammis, a pair of wrestlers trying to shed their "bad guy" image. (CHAMP)

Baxter

After Sam leaped into Ron Miller, this wounded veteran began hallucinating that Charlie (the enemy) was coming, even though they were in a veteran's hospital in the States. (NOWHERE)

Bean, Dr. T.

A Texas panhandle veterinarian Sam called on when Christie Dalton started to wheeze. She charged Sam and Bunny $30 for the visit. (MAYBE)

Beatles, The

Sam leaped into New York City just days before the Fab Four were to appear on *The Ed Sullivan Show*. He was blinded by a photographer's flashbulb while the press and fans were converging on the group in front of the La Fronchette Diner. (BLIND)

Beaumont, Annie Klebbard

Billy's sister-in-law was going to leave her husband for his brother if Sam didn't do something. (RAIN)

Beaumont, William (Billy)

His trailer read, "William Beaumont, Ph.D., Purveyor of prescription and maker of rain. Dr. of Meteorology and Climatology." In short, the man was a rainmaker, and Sam leaped into him just in time to drive into Beaumont's home town of Clover Bend, Texas, where Ziggy says it won't rain for another eight months, four days, two hours and 44 minutes. (RAIN)

Beaumont, Clint

Sleazy photographer who wormed his way into being official photographer for the Miss Deep South pageant. His speciality was luring young girls into dropping their inhibitions and then some for photographs he later sold. (SOUTH)

Beaumont, Grace

Billy Beaumont's mother. (RAIN)

Beaumont, Ralph

He believed his brother Billy was a fraud. Actually, he probably resented staying at home while Billy toured the country. He was about to lose his wife Annie because he worked so hard on the farm and the family business that he neglected her. (RAIN)

Beche, Tony

San Francisco psychic Tamlyn Matsuda identified him as the killer of Janine Travis. (EYES)

Beckett, Grandma Nettie

At least we'll assume she was a Beckett until we're told otherwise. She drank decaf coffee. A jar of the stuff was still in the Beckett pantry in 1969 when Sam tried to get his dad to do something about his lifestyle. (HOME)

Beckett, Grandpa

He died when he was 57, a sign of things to come for John Beckett. (HOME)

Beckett, John, Captain, Army of the Potomac

Sam's great-grandfather fought in the battle of Antietam in the Civil War and got separated from the main army. Taken in by a slave, John fell in love with Olivia Covington, a widow who nursed him to health. In a bizarre twist on Sam's own string theory, he found he could leap along his own DNA when he found himself as John Beckett. (STATES)

Beckett, John Samuel

Sam's father, who was named after his grandfather (STATES), was a kind man who never once degraded his wife Thelma (LIBERATION).

By 1969, he was starting to get deaf from all those years on a tractor. When Sam leaped home, he said his father would die in 1972. He smoked Luckies and claimed he was healthy because he worked hard, slept good and ate plenty of dairy products.

When Sam found himself in his home town in 1971, John was still alive, working the farm 16 hours a day, seven days a week. Despite all his hard work, the farm still got taken away from him and may have been one factor eventually contributing to his death. (LAND)

He died either in 1973 or 1974 of a heart attack. (PILOT, FREEDOM)

Also the name of John's uncle who lives in Australia. Sam masqueraded as Uncle John's son named Sam when he called home from Waco, TX (PILOT).

Beckett, Katherine (Katie)

Sam's sister was born in 1957. She got married for the first time at the age of 17, mainly because she wanted to get away from the farm. Her husband Chuck abused her, but she was too afraid to leave and too ashamed to tell anyone about him. She eventually did get out of the marriage, and later married Jim Bonnick, a Naval officer. They now live in Hawaii with their two children and Thelma Beckett. (PILOT, CAM)

Beckett, Samuel

Born August 8, 1953 at 12:30 p.m. in Elk Ridge, Indiana. Social security : 563-86-9801. DOD UMBRA Clearance : 004-02-016. Driver's Licence : 5738457, expires 1998. Height: 6′ 0″. Weight: 175 pounds. Hair: Brown. Eyes: Green. Address: P.O. Box 555, Stallions Springs, New Mexico 87901-4093. (MIRROR, BRIGHT)

At an early age Sam showed he was gifted. He could read at the age of two, do calculus in his head at the age of five, and at ten was able to beat a computer at chess. (HONEYMOON)

He took his first train ride at the age of two, and he remembered being confused, frightened and sure everyone was out to get him. His mother gave him a book to calm him down (HONEYMOON). When Sam was four, he wrote to Captain Galaxy, asking him about his theory of time travel (FUTURE).

Despite being so exceptional, Sam remembers having a fairly normal childhood. Like any kid, he fought with his brother and sister, calling it the law of sibling survival (MOTHER). He also followed his older brother Tom around like a puppy, and the two were very close (HOME).

When Sam was nine, Tom took him to see a Tarzan movie. Afterward they went home to play Tarzan, swinging on a rope tied to a beam in the barn. The knot loosened, and Tom sent Sam up to tighten it. He froze after he climbed up, and ever since has had a fear of heights (NET). That Christmas his dad gave him a sled, and he and Tom spent the day playing out in the snow (MIRACLE). Sam was learning to drive a tractor when he learned of the death of president Kennedy (LHO).

A voracious reader, Sam counted *Brigadoon* (TRILOGY) and *Who Killed Grimsley and Allen?* (SEYMOUR) among the books he read as a child. He also used to memorize train timetables, which must have been easy considering he has a photographic memory (CATCH). While Sam spend some time in Indian Guides (SHREW), he never had a paper route. Sam is a pretty good shot, having learned from hunting pheasants as a youth (HOME).

He remembers being smart and shy at the age of fifteen (MOTHER). That was also the year he had a crush on Nicole, his piano teacher. She left to attend Julliard, but Sam met up with her on a later leap (CATCH). Like many children who are gifted in math, Sam was also gifted in music. His first piano teacher, Mrs. Greenberg, left because she couldn't teach him any more. At the age of nineteen, he played piano at Carnegie Hall (BLIND).

Sam's parents had a profound effect on his life, teaching him about the evils of prejudice (JUSTICE) and dealing discipline fairly and firmly (MOTHER). He felt lucky

23

growing up with parents who would listen to him (8½). In fact, he and his father often had heart-to-heart talks over a game of ping-pong (MOTHER). His father also taught him the names of the constellations, fostering a life-long interest in astronomy. John Beckett felt that if Sam knew the names of the stars above his home, he would never be alone because he could always look up and know that his parents were looking at the same stars (SHREW).

Another childhood interest was Egyptology. He couldn't believe that there was anything as old as the pyramids, and loved to study them (CURSE).

The family had no dogs, but did have two cats named Donner and Blitzen (STROBE).

Sam used to love it when the circus came to town (NET), and also liked to go to the store with his dad. He would get two sticks of cinnamon and his dad two sticks of peppermint (FREEDOM).

While talented athletically, Sam was not as good as his brother Tom. He played basketball in high school, and Tom talked him out of taking a basketball scholarship at Indiana State and into studying physics. This was after a conversation with a professor at MIT (possibly Sebastian LoNigro), during which Tom was told that a brain like Sam's only comes along once in a generation. At the time, Sam was weighing offers from a dozen universities, and Cal Tech was on the list along with Indiana (DISCO, HOME).

During Thanksgiving of 1969, the entire family was together for the last time. Tom was on his way to Vietnam and would die in April of the next year. Sam leaped into himself at this time and tried to change history, but the more he tried, the more his family thought there was something wrong. They even called in the doctor, who said Sam was just under a lot of pressure. The real reason Sam was there was to win a basketball game. After he won, he leaped into his brother's S.E.A.L. unit and save his life. (HOME, NAM)

In the fall of 1970, Sam went away to college. He may have taken some courses for college credit while he was in high school, but he still went through four years of MIT in two, and became the youngest ever to graduate *summa cum laude*. In the summer of 1973 he and professor Sebastian LoNigro worked out the String Theory in the latter's cabin in the Berkshires (CHARM).

While in college Sam never joined a fraternity because he thought everyone seemed to be such pigs. He hated piles of clothes and the smell of stale beer. When he leaped into a fraternity rat, he had a lot of trouble coping with the situation. Al told Sam it was because he didn't know how to have fun; that his idea of fun was studying ancient languages and quantum physics. In short, he was a meganerd (FRAT). Later, Sam called college a four-year license to learn and have fun without the pressures of family (RETURN).

Sam continued to acquire degrees, and now he holds seven doctorates. Five of them are in Quantum Physics (PILOT, CROSSED), Medicine (PILOT, CROSSED), Music (SONG), Archaeology (CURSE: his thesis was on Ptah-Hotep) and Ancient Languages (CROSSED). We know he doesn't hold degrees in Law (he admitted he learned all he knows about the subject from watching *Perry Mason* on TV) (HELP) and Psychiatry. It's quite probable one of his doctorates is in Artificial Intelligence, since he designed Ziggy and the breakthrough technology needed to make the computer possible (PILOT).

Besides his many degrees, Sam Beckett speaks seven modern languages (CROSSED), including French (BRIDE), Japanese (MACHIKO), German (HEART) and Spanish (ALL, WONDERFUL), and four dead ones. Russian does not seem to be on the list, as he surprised himself by speaking it when he leaped into Lee Harvey Oswald (LHO). Sam also does not speak Hebrew (SHALT), Italian (DOUBLE) or Hungarian (NET). Al helped him on those three.

John Beckett died when Sam was 21, and Sam carried a load of guilt around for the rest of his life because he was not able to be there for his family. (FREEDOM, LAND)

Sam never went on a job interview until he leaped into Jimmy LaMotta (JIMMY), so he was probably recruited for any jobs on the basis of his reputation. Al brought him on to the Star Bright Project about the time Donna Elesee was leaving. Sam and Donna fell in love and, as Sam remembered, they were going to get married at the Old Mission Chapel on the fifth of June, but she left him at the altar. During a leap to Lawrence College in 1972, Sam spied a young Donna and attempted to change history. When he and Al simo-leaped and he briefly came home, Sam remembered that Donna was his wife. (BALL, CROSSED, BACK)

Sam and Al first met in the lab at Star Bright. Al was beating a vending machine with a hammer because it had eaten his dime. He was drunk and angry and on the verge of being washed out of the project. Sam saw that there was a terrific person inside and went to bat for Al, helping him through what had to be one of the toughest times of his life. The pair became best friends, and Al repaid the favor by helping fight for funding for Project Quantum Leap. (BALL)

Sam says he created PQL in 1995, but that is more like the date of his first leap. Before that were years of design and construction. He and Al built the Imaging Chamber themselves, and during that time the cast recording of *The Man of La Mancha* was the only CD Sam played. (CATCH)

Sam felt that no one believed in Project Quantum Leap, and he had to tell himself not to listen to others (BLIND). He believes that great scientists are never objective, which is why people think they're loony. The first time Sam realized his time travel calculations were working, he felt unbelievably lucky to be there on the cutting edge of solving one of mankind's oldest riddles. He felt the same way later when he saw a UFO. (BRIGHT)

Sam's idol is Albert Einstein (NORMA), and *Time* magazine once called Sam Beckett "the next Einstein". Sam also has a Nobel Prize, presumably for physics work related to the Project. (PILOT, WRONG, DISCO)

Reflecting his solid Midwesten upbringing, Sam operates by a "traditional" set of morals. At various times Al has called him names such as "The Prudent Prince" and "Mr. Morals". Naturally, they do clash on topics such as sex. Sam believes in a woman's right to choose her own lifestyle (GLORIA), and also doesn't believe he should sleep with a woman unless he loves her. On the other hand, he seems to have a habit of falling for women he meets. Sleeping with another man's wife is a big personal taboo (HELP).

Indeed, Sam is prudish. He's had trouble saying the word "breasts" on more than on occasion. He did, however, balk at signing a Declaration of Purity contract while a beauty contestant. He felt that sort of thing shouldn't make any difference. (SOUTH)

As the beauty contestant, he had what he said was the most humiliating experience of his life when he had to dress as Carmen Miranda and sing "Cuanda La Gusta" (SOUTH). On the other hand, he said virtually the same thing when he leaped into a Chippendales dancer and found himself mobbed by fans (DANCER). Sam made similar comments when he was a rock singer caught in a "fan sandwich" (ROCK).

Al also calls Sam terminally good, and characterizes him as a Boy Scout, but the truth is that Sam actually does want to help people and "put right what was once went wrong". As Roberto Gutierrez, he said he saw himself as "the champion of underdogs everywhere" (ROBERTO).

Sam has a variety of skills that have been very useful, in

his travels, and he's often a quick student of skills he doesn't have, thanks to his photographic memory (CATCH, SOUTH, POOL, PIANO, PLAY). Along with the aforementioned piano talent, he also plays guitar (both acoustic and electric) and can play a variety of styles (SHALT, HOME, ROCK, BRIGHT, MEMPHIS). When he leaped into a Mafia hit man, he found out he could sing (DOUBLE), and since then has done everything from gospel to musicals to Elvis. As a consequence of leaping, Sam has holes in his memory concerning musicians. He has remembered and forgotten John Lennon, and when Al asked him if he remembered Pete Townsend, Sam's reply was "Who?" Al's answer: "Right." (ROCK, HOME).

Sam is mechanically inclined, having designed and built the Imaging Chamber. He can also listen to a car and tell what is wrong with it (CAM). While a DJ at WOF in Peoria, he fixed the station console, generator and transmission line (PEORIA).

Physically, Sam is very fit. Apparently he once did aerobic dancing, as he tried to lead the Cougars football team in an exercise to 'La Bamba' (ALL). He's also very adept in martial arts. Among his specialities are judo, karate, tae kwon do, sabatt and mu tai (MOTHER).

As a child of the microwave age, Sam is a fair cook. He does good simple breakfasts like eggs and bacon, and cooks griddlecakes using his mom's recipe. Anything more complicated, and he usually manages to burn or otherwise ruin the dish. The one exception seems to have been when, as his great-grandfather, he cooked up a fairly serviceable dinner for Olivia Covington. (STROBE, LIBERATION, MOTHER, SOUTH).

One skill Sam never learned was how to fly an airplane. His first leap was into a test pilot, and Al talked him through the flight, but had Sam bail our because the landing would have been too complicated. A second time when Sam was a pilot, Al helped him some with the controls, but Sam generally freezes up in a cockpit. (PILOT, SHIP)

Sam's favourite drinks seem to be dry beer, Evian and hot tea – especially orange spice. A favorite dish is a cheeseburger, cooked medium rare with no tomato and extra onions. Sam also likes the theatre, and his favorite Marilyn Monroe film is *Some Like it Hot*. (NORMA)

While Sam enjoys music, he hates disco (DISCO). In fact, he would rather die. He doesn't seem to be a big fan of rap, but he did program a rap tune into Ziggy (SHOCK). A big Elvis Presley fan, Sam not only programmed all of The King's hits into the computer's memory banks, but he used to sing Elvis songs for days and drive Al crazy (MEMPHIS).

Sam's favorite method of relaxation is with a light beer, microwave popcorn and a movie in the VCR (GLORIA). The only things he takes seriously are quantum physics and time travel, or so he told Rachel Porter (PEORIA).

Al told Sam he sweated at his wedding – just kidding. (Or was he?) (MACHIKO). Sam also says he would marry the right someone after knowing her just a couple of hours (HURRICANE), and has repeatedly said he would like to have a family (NORMA, SHALT). That wish was granted when he fathered a child by Abagail Fuller. Sammie Jo Fuller does not know who her father is, but she now works at PQL and has a theory on how to bring Sam Beckett home (TRILOGY).

When Sam landed at Al's Place in Cokeburg, PA, he told the bartender that his one regret was that he did not change Al Calavicci's life for the better by saving his marriage to Beth. Then he leaped to Beth in 1969 (as himself, not in another persona) and told her that Al was coming home. Even so, Sam himself still has not made it home. (MIRROR)

Beckett, Thelma Louise

Sam's mother. In 1967, her pumpkin pie had taken a blue
ribbon at the Elk Ridge County Fair for the previous ten
years (PILOT). Sam also recalled that she made the best
strawberry shortcake (JUSTICE). Thelma now lives in
Hawaii with Katie and her husband (PILOT). Sam remembered that his dad never once denigrated his mom,
and she thought women's lib was probably a good thing –
for other women (LIBERATION).

Beckett, Thomas, Lieutenant (US Navy)

Sam's older brother was a gifted athlete and made All-
State in high school and played in the state basketball
championships of 1964. Of course, he played for Elk
Ridge, and regretted that Bentleyville was the one team
they couldn't beat. He graduated from Annapolis in 1969
and finished his S.E.A.L. training just before Thanksgiving of that same year. Tom talked Sam out of accepting
a basketball scholarship at Indiana State, presumably after
speaking with LoNigro. His pet name for Sam is "little
brother". In the original history, Tom died on April 8,
1970 in Vietnam. Sam got to change that.

Tom had led a S.E.A.L. squadron over to Vietnam in
December of 1969. The Bravo squad had been on tour of
duty for five months when Sam leaped into "Magic", their
radio man. After Magic saved his life, Tom put his arm
around him and said, "Thanks, little brother." When Sam
leaped back to his home town in December of 1971, he was
told that Tom had just returned from Vietnam. (HOME,
NAM, DISCO)

Becky

A girl from Wichita who had hitched herself up with the Cobras motorcycle gang, and in particular with Dillon, their leader. She wanted to be a writer, and felt that being on the road was the only way to experience life so she could write. (REBEL)

Beederman, Sam

A case of acute depression got this man committed to Havenwell Hospital, and Sam leaped in just in time to receive a shock treatment. The dosage was much higher than normal, which sent Sam's mind spinning off on a journey from which it almost never returned. (SHOCK)

Beeks, Verbena

When Al first mentioned her, Sam thought the observer was talking about tranquilizers. In fact, she's the project psychiatrist. Al used to think she was cute, but seems to have little use for her observations most of the time. (GLORIA)

Beeman, Frederick R.

Editor of the *Peoria Dispatch* and self-appointed moralist about town, he tried everything within his means to stop WOF from playing rock and roll music. (PEORIA)

Bellini, Nick

Grew up with Joey DeNardo in Chicago. While Joey got into music, Nick got into the mob and eventually used Joey to set up another childhood friend named Ponti so

Nick could murder the latter man. Joey ran away and changed his name, but Nick used Lorraine, Joey's fiancée, to track him down by pretending to have a romantic interest in her. (PIANO)

Bellisario, Don

The future QL producer met Lee Harvey Oswald while in the Marines and used that scene in the LHO leap. (LHO)

Benning, Carol

An inmate at the Mallard prison who was killed just before Sam and Alia leaped into Liz Tate and Angel Jenson. The pair had been accused of the murder. Her death turned out to have been caused by abortion complications after she had been impregnated by the warden. (REVENGE)

Bentenhoff, Ike

Works in Imaging Control at Project Quantum Leap. Al said that when he and Lucille snuck into the Energizing Chamber to "exchange Christmas gifts" at a party, Ike "took advantage" of Tina. (TESS)

Bentleyville Tigers

In the original history, they beat the Elk Ridge Cougars in 1969. Elk Ridge always opened the season with a game against Bentleyville the day after Thanksgiving. That day became a turning point in a lot of lives. If the Cougars won, they would go to the State Championship. The coach would eventually get a job at Iowa and go on to the NBA. The state championship meant scholarships for several people who probably wouldn't have gone to college otherwise. (HOME)

Bianca, Frank

Ran a Beverley Hills beauty salon simply called Bianca. He was *the* hairdresser in Beverly Hills, but his name used to be Maurice Lipschitz. (PERM)

Bibi

The lovely maid who worked for Michael Blake. (MIRACLE)

Bigfoot

Creature of legend who is generally sighted in mountains and wooded areas. Sam and Al spotted one after Karen Marlet's truck had been mysteriously moved from a pile of rocks on which it had lodged and turned back in the direction of the town. (BEAST)

Bigley, Frank

Engaged to Sue Ann Winters, he acted like he owned his intended, discouraging her from pursuing a singing career. His family owned Bigley's Shoe Factory in Louisville. (MEMPHIS)

Billings, Dorothy Louise (Dotty)

She operated a beauty salon out of her home and gave Billie Jean Crockett a job there while she was pregnant. She didn't want to commit to letting the girl stay on after the baby was born because she was afraid of losing her boyfriend Keeter. She ended up marrying Billie Jean's father

Bob – who had been her old high school sweetheart – and the two of them helped Billie Jean look after the baby. (8½)

Billings, Marie

Housekeeper for the Fuller Family for 30 years. In 1978, Marie went to Larry Stanton/Sam and asked him to defend Abagail Fuller in the murder of Leta Aider. Stanton originally didn't take the case. (TRILOGY)

Billy C.

The sax-playing president made a brief appearance at the Southern Salute to America talent show in 1954. (MEM-PHIS)

Billy Wayne

Bat boy for the Galveston Mustangs. He caught Bunny Twilly trying to come on to Doc Fuller/Sam. (BALL)

Bingo (the game)

Sam as Don Geno had to help Nona win at Bingo before he could leap out. (DOUBLE)

Bingo (the person)

Al's nickname as a young pilot. When Sam leaped into him in June 1957, Bingo was 23. Bingo got his nickname while on a cross-country trip. His plane sprang an oil leak, and he had to make a forced landing, hitting his head as he came down. He thought he had concussion at first. The next morning his buddies found him asleep under the wing. When they asked about how he spent the night, he replied, "Bingo, bango, bongo." Back at the Project,

Bingo thought Al was his uncle Jack, plus he had the hots for Tina. (LISA)

Bionic Woman, The

Diana Frost's favorite TV show. (HUNT)

Bird Dog

Pilot slang for the radio location system on an aircraft. Sam had to learn to use one when he flew through the Bermuda Triangle. (SHIP)

Birdell, Captain Tom "Bird Dog"

Tom Stratton's best friend and fellow X-2 pilot. The nickname "Bird Dog" was given because he was constantly chasing women. (PILOT)

Black Mamba

One of the deadliest snakes in the world. Writer Joshua Rey kept one as a pet. It later got loose and killed Dorothy Yeager. (BMAN)

Blake, Michael

A multi-millionaire who got his money by putting people out of work. He started out buying small mom-and-pop companies, automating them, and then selling them for a nice profit. By 1962, he had worked up to doing it with larger businesses. His pet project was Blake Plaza, and he was determined to evict a street mission in order to erect the structure. Because his brainwaves were on a frequency similar to Sam's, he could see Al. Sam and Al did a "Scrooge" on Blake, convincing him to change his ways.

He did erect Blake Plaza, but put the street mission on the ground floor, and married the lady who ran it. (MIRACLE)

Blake Plaza

Millionaire Michael Blake planned to build the ultimate Manhattan skyscraper with the most contemporary theatres, shops and offices in all of New York. If he had continued along his greedy path, the building would have been bought out by the Japanese and renamed Sumoto Plaza. (MIRACLE)

Blakowski, Michael

Michael Blake's real name. (MIRACLE)

Blanchette, Reta

Laura Fuller's mother killed all of her children except Laura after she lost her husband and her money. Then she cut her own throat. The local story was that she would rather kill her babies than see them starve. Mr. Devereux, who found the carnage, said she'd lost her mind. The local legend had it that the family had one cursed child every generation. First Reta, then Laura, now Abagail. Later it came out the reason Laura wasn't killed is that she had slipped down between the beds and was not seen by her mother. (TRILOGY)

Blaster

The S.E.A.L. Tom's unit pulled through the delta on a slalom ski behind a helicopter. (NAM)

Blood Moon

A sacred night that occurs once every ten years when the walking dead honor the name of Count Bathory. (BLOOD)

Blue Mamba Club

Harry Spontini was working this Oakland night spot in 1974 when Sam leaped in. (SPONT)

'Blue Moon of Kentucky'

Elvis Presley sang this and 'That's All Right, Momma' in the original history for Mr. Phillips of Sun Records. (MEMPHIS)

Boardman, Dennis

Sam leaped into Marilyn Monroe's driver on April 4, 1960. His job was to keep her from dying from a drug overdose so she could make one last film – *The Misfits*. (NORMA)

Bobo

Sam leaped into this "chimponaut" in contention to be the first chimp in space. Bobo wore the number 52. Al theorized Sam was able to make the leap because, genetically, chimps are 99% identical to humans. Lemon drops were Bobo's favorite treat, and his favorite protein was caterpillars. (WRONG)

Boface

Cissy Davis' dog. She originally died going back to her house to save him during hurricane Camille, but Sam went to the rescue instead. (HURRICANE)

Bonnick, Lieutenant (US Navy) Jim,

Katie's husband. Kate and Jim live in Hawaii with Sam's mom and their two kids. He's stationed at Pearl Harbor. (PILOT)

Boogieman, The

When Sam first leaped, his brain was so scrambled he thought he was having a nightmare and Al was the Boogieman. (PILOT) Also the title of the Halloween episode of the third season, where the Devil took the form of Al. Sam had a number of clues that the Al that appeared to him was not Al;

1. He had a handlink, but Ziggy never knew much of anything.
2. Mary felt Al's presence (although that has happened before, so that isn't a clue in and of itself).
3. He never used the Imaging Chamber door.
4. He was not spooked by Joshua Rey's gruesomely decorated office, or the black cat which unexpectedly jumped on his desk.
5. He may have caused a skull to fly across the room, rather than Mary Greely.
6. When he and Sam visited Mary Greely's house at 966 Salem Avenue, the 9 turned upside-down as Al walked through the doorway.
7. He coughed on Al's cigar.

8. He suggested to Sam that "the Boogieman" committed the murders.

9. He didn't have his link out when he told Gooshie to center him on Mary.

10. He quoted Tully's line about them that dance with the Devil, although he wasn't present when Tully spoke it.

11. He never walked through anything.

12. He was the only other person around when Dorothy and Tully died. When he was finally asked about his identity, he told Sam, "Yin and Yang Good and Bad. God . . ."

"The Devil," Sam replied.

"In the flesh, so to speak." Later he added, "Who gave you the right to go bungling around in time, putting right what I made wrong?" (BMAN)

Boone, Jasper

Unjustly accused of an armed robbery at a jewelry store, he's serving fifteen years on a road crew at the Tallawaga County Prison. Jasper told Sam that his father was a colored farmer from North Carolina, and his mother was a full-bloodied Muskogee Indian. After his parents died in a fire, he was brought up on the reservation by his grandmother. As a result, he loves the open spaces and tends to get claustrophobic when in a tight area. After Sam helped him escape, Boone vanished, but three years later a man answering his description was seen in Washington State, working for the forestry service. (UNCHAINED)

Boorman's Frosty Freeze Ice Cream

Sam totally botched up a commercial for this establishment when he leaped in at WOF radio. (PEORIA)

Bowers

Judge in Kevin Wentworth's trial on the charge of raping Katie McBain. (RAPED)

Bowman

Florida governor who issued a stay of execution for Jesus Ortega. (LAST)

Boxer Boy Underwear

"Lasts a lifetime plus ten years." Al still owns a pair. (PLAY)

Brackett, Ed (Francis Edward)

Young corporate jet co-pilot whom Al called a "fledging airborne limo driver". His plane was going to vanish in the Bermuda Triangle. (SHIP)

Brenda

The redhead in coding that got turned on by the dirty pictures Gooshie had Ziggy printing at the party to celebrate Sam's successful leap. Al took her into the filing room later. (PILOT)

Brengle, Dwayne

Promoter/manager of the rock group King Thunder, he was "investing" the band members' money and giving them access to very little of it. Apparently he was losing more money in the stock market than he made in a year, and was embezzling money from the band to cover his losses. When Dwayne realized Tonic/Sam was catching on to his scheme he dressed as a deranged fan and tried to kill him. (ROCK)

Brewster, Susan

A white Los Angeles medical student who was dating Ray Harper of Watts. Ray's brother Lonnie took her as a hostage during the Watts riots and promised to kill her if another black person died. Susan and Ray graduated from med school, married, and set up a clinic in Watts. (B&W)

Brian

DJ at WOF who had the shift after Chick Howell. (PEORIA)

Bridges, Doug

Announcer on Dr. Ruth Westheimer's radio program. He and producer Debbie Schafer had an on-again, off-again relationship. Sam got Doug and Debbie together for good by letting them air their feelings on the air. (RUTH)

Brown, Max

Ohio senator, father of Diane McBride and golfing buddy of President Eisenhower. Senator Brown died in 1965, and in the original history the man who won his seat (possibly Weitzman) became the Commitee chairman. After Sam altered history, he was replaced by Diane McBride. (HONEYMOON)

Brown, Roy

Vietnam vet living in a wooded mountain camp with his friend Henry Adams. Brown had been a "tunnel rat" in the war, crawling into small spaces to spy on the enemy. He took a bullet in the head, and as a result had hallucinations and seizures. (BEAST)

Brownfield, Evy

One of two people George Sanders was considering promoting. Even though she had a year of seniority, her gender was holding her back. And even if she did get the promotion, it would be at a lower salary. Sam encouraged her to tell George about her ideas if she was really serious about getting that promotion. She did, and ended up not only getting the promotion, but full pay as well. (LIBERATION)

Bruckner, Kevin

Typical fifteen-year-old boy into "Demons and Dragons" and girls. He ran away from his friends after they set him up to admit he was a virgin, and was kidnapped while riding his bike down a dark road. Linda/Sam rescued him. (MOTHER)

Bruckner, Linda

Her husband ran off with another woman, and she bounced back and got her real-estate license and was trying to keep her children's lives normal. (MOTHER)

Bruckner, Susan

Kevin's eleven-year-old sister. When Sam leaped in, the two were fighting over a Queen T-shirt, which they subsequently ripped in half. (MOTHER)

Bruckner, Teresa

Kevin's little sister. because she's under five, she sees Sam as "a strange man dressed in Mommy's clothes". He and Al convinced the frightened child that they were there to help Kevin, and that her mother would be back in a couple of days. In the meantime, she strikes up a friendship with "Angel Al". (MOTHER)

Bryant, Dr. Gerald

A boozed-out literature professor at Lawrence College who was about to be forced into a shotgun wedding with Jamie Lee, one of his students. They were having an affair. In his book (which he may have written just to pick up coeds) he wrote: "Between love and the noblest cause there should be no contest. Love is the only true satisfaction." (CROSSED)

Bubbles

Budd Wright's poodle. (GLORIA)

Buffalo Chimps

Chimps dressed as cowboys were the big attraction at Wild Willy's Western World, and Butchie Rickett had been bugging his dad for weeks about going to se them.

Now that Sam was Butchie, he wasn't exactly thrilled with the idea. (RUNAWAY)

Bunch, Velton and the Dovetones

Group heard over KCB radio in the pilot. In reality, Bunch wrote the music for the series. (PILOT)

Burch, Cheryl Lynn

She was Miss Mason-Dixon Line in the Miss Deep South contest. Her goals were to become a professional secretary and to have many children. She placed third. (SOUTH)

Burger, Dr.

One of the officers in charge of the supersonic flight program at Edwards Air Force Base.

A different Dr. Burger was the base doctor where Al was an ensign. (LISA)

And yet another was the Beckett family physician. (HOME)

Burke, Daniel

When this boy saw Henry Adams/Sam he was convinced he saw Bigfoot. The mistake may have been easy to make in the dark, as Adams wore a huge furry-hooded coat and had a copious beard. Daniel wanted to prove the legendary monster existed, and nearly died doing so. (BEAST)

Burke, John

Of four high school buddies that went to Vietnam, John Burke never returned. He was killed when his friend and subordinate Luke Marlet refused to go inside a hooch and kill an old man, although they were under orders to secure the village. No one knew the hooch was booby trapped, and when John went in, it exploded. He left a wife and a son. (BEAST)

Burma Shave

Peg Stratton bought some for her husband Tom because the PX was out of his regular brand. Sam was thoroughly befuddled because he was used to an electric razor. Later they saw a series of the famous signs:
    Why is it
    When you
    Try to pass
    The guy in front
    Goes twice as fast?
    BURMA SHAVE
(PILOT)

Burt

The doorman at the building where Michael Blake had a penthouse apartment. (MIRACLE)

Buster

A bouncer at the Girls A-Go-Go lounge, Sam found himself in Buster's life as he and Bunny O-Hare kidnapped a baby. (MAYBE)

Butcher

Abusive orderly at Havenwell Hospital who gave Sam Beederman an electroshock treatment because the patient hit him. Sam Beckett had just leaped into Beederman when the shock was administered. (SHOCK)

C

Calavicci, Albert, Admiral (US Navy)

Born June 15, 1934 (BACK, LISA) to an Italian father and a mother of Russian ancestry. Al had a sister named Trudy, who suffered from Down's Syndrome. When he was a child, his mother ran off with an encyclopedia salesman, and Al felt part of the reason she left was the pressure of raising Trudy. But while he could forgive her for leaving her husband, he could never forgive her for leaving her children behind. (JIMMY, RUNAWAY)

Al's father was from the Abruzzi section of Italy – a regular "Hopalong Cassadich". He was a construction worker, and after his wife left he placed the children in an orphanage while he worked a variety of jobs, eventually ending up in Saudi Arabia. Whenever he was in town, he would go to the orphanage on weekends and sneak his son out for Chianti and risotto. (DOUBLE)

After he returned from the Middle East, he had saved enough money to buy a small house. Al later recalled that it was the greatest house he'd seen. The family was together and happy, but the happiness was brief, for when Al was eleven, his father took very ill with cancer. The family were devout Catholics, and his father asked Al to pray for his healing. "Don't worry," he told his son, "everything will be all right as long as you pray for me." Al prayed at church every day, praying his heart out until his father died. After that, Al broke with the church and held a grudge against it for many years. (FAITH)

After his father's death, the two children went back to an orphanage. Trudy became ill and was taken to an institution. (It should be noted here that Al has also mentioned that Trudy never went to the orphanage, that she was always in an institution, save the brief time the three of them were together.) (JIMMY, EVIL, FAITH)

Al tells many stories of his days in the orphanage. When he was eight, he had a pet cockroach named Kevin (NET). He also acquired the nickname "Al the Pick", presumably for his lock-picking skills (SPONT).

At the age of ten, he ran away from the orphanage and became so cold and hungry and desperate that he tried to pick someone's pocket. Fortunately for him, that someone was the legendary pool player Charlie "Black Magic" Walters. Instead of turning Al in, he took the boy under his wing and, declaring that children should have a family, tried to find one for the boy. They traveled together for months, Al learning how to shoot pool and winning Walter's trust to such an extent that he was allowed to shoot with Alberta, the player's legendary cue. Magic was eventually busted for playing in a whites-only hall, and Al was sent back to the orphanage. That short period had a profound effect on him, as he claimed Walters turned his life around and showed him that there were indeed people who cared. (POOL)

One of his worst childhood memories was at the age of fifteen, being busted by a girl's parents just as he was about to put the make on her (MOTHER). But sixteen was the happiest time of his life. He had three girls alone in the orphanage, or so he claimed (ALL). As a teenager Al was also a regional Golden Gloves champion at the age of 16

(HAND), and at one point he ran away to join the circus (NET). His ticket out, however, was the theatre (CATCH).

After he left the orphanage, he went to the institution to get Trudy, and was told that she had died at the age of sixteen of pneumonia. Al was shattered by the news. At this point everyone he loved had left him. (JIMMY)

He went on to college, attending both MIT and the Naval Academy, though we are not sure in what order. Al was quite a prankster in college (FRAT), and also spoke of Bebop and a Lithuanian named Danese getting him through long nights at MIT (PILOT). He played baseball in the Navy, wearing the number 9. He was the team's starting pitcher and had the best earned run average in the league (BALL). At graduation, he was in charge of tapping the kegs (HONOR).

By the age of 23 he was an Ensign in the Navy and a fighter pilot stationed at Pensacola, where he picked up the nickname "Bingo". In 1957 he was arrested on the charge of murdering Marci Riker, the wife of his commanding officer, but was released after his girlfriend Lisa Sherman stepped forward and said the two of them were together the night of the murder. After she told the authorities, she died in a car wreck. Lt. Sherman was a nurse at the base, and was also married. Sam leaped into Al's life at this time, and told Lisa not to testify. It also put him in the position of having to prove his friend's innocence. (LISA)

It was probably during this period that he went on civil rights marches and developed his taste for chitlins (COLOR). He also attended several small black churches (SONG).

In 1958 he met the legendary author Jack Kerouac. It was during Al's pledge year at Annapolis, and the author gave a reading at St John's College, and Al and some of his friends attended and afterward partied with the legendary beat writer. Al claims the book *On the Road* changed his life. (REBEL)

It was probably during this period that he made frequent trips to New York to visit friends who were photographers. (STROBE)

Al was stationed in Japan at one point, and was able to make use of his knowledge of customs when Sam leaped into Charlie MacKenzie (MACHIKO). Whenever he went out on liberty, he would take the precaution of hiding money in his shoes in case he got drunk (PERM). At one point he didn't seem to give much thought to advancement in the Navy, considering anyone above the rank of lieutenant to be a horse's ass. Albert Calavicci eventually rose to the rank of Admiral (MIA, HONEYMOON).

Around 1961, he married Beth, a Navy nurse (MIA, MIRROR). During the Cuban Missile Crisis, he flew reconnaissance flights in an F-4 Phantom escort over the island nation. After one of their U-2's got shot down, his squadron went in. Later he said he didn't know at the time how close they came to World War III. (NUCLEAR)

When the war in Vietnam escalated, he went as a fighter pilot. He was based on a ship, and in 1967 his A-4 went down over the highlands. Al was kept imprisoned in a cage near Cham Hoi until after the U.S. pulled out in 1973. Physically, he subsisted on weevil-infested rice and what rainwater he could catch in his mouth. He also said his love for Beth kept him alive (MIA). In April of 1970, he was nearly repatriated during an abortive rescue attempt by a S.E.A.L. unit. Because Sam had leaped into the unit (led by Sam's brother Tom), photographer Maggie Dawson caught a dramatic photograph of Al that won her a posthumous Pulitzer Prize (NAM). After Al was repatriated, he found that his wife had declared him dead and married a lawyer named Dirk Simon (MIA).

After Vietnam came a period with NASA, during which Al circled the moon ten times and read from the book of *Genesis* during one Apollo mission (WRONG). The 1970s were among Al's happiest times. With the space program behind him and the Starbright Project ahead of him, his 100% virgin polyester suit got him almost as many women as did his space suit. He roamed the discos wearing his "man bag" and picking up women (DISCO).

Al hit bottom while assigned to the Starbright Project. By this time he was drinking heavily and was probably depressed over flying a desk rather than an airplane or spacecraft. While he had just brought a bring young quantum physicist on board, he was drunk and angry and the government was ready to wash him out of the Project – and probably the Navy – completely. One day when he was taking his anger out on a vending machine with a hammer because it had eaten his dime, Sam Beckett arrived at the lab. Sam perceived that underneath all that booze and anger was a terrific person, and he went to bat for his superior (BALL). The pair became fast friends, and when Sam started Project Quantum Leap, Al was there for him: going to bat for funding (HONEYMOON), helping to build the accelerator (CATCH), and becoming Sam's observer. By September 18, 1999, Al had saved Sam's life 23 times (BACK).

Admiral Calavicci is known for his womanizing ways, and his list of female companions is almost legendary. He's been married five times, and spent his first, third and fifth honeymoons at Niagara Falls. (HONEYMOON)

Beth was Al's first wife, and according to him, the only woman he ever really loved; the only woman he ever wanted to grow old with. "If you're lucky life is gonna give you one shot at true love", he told Sam, "and Beth was mine." (MIA). At first he described her to Sam as a redhead "who could make Father Flanigan forget about Boys' Town."(SEYMOUR). When Sam leaped into a policeman in April 1969 and met Beth, she had brown hair (MIA).

They were married for eight years, but spent less than two of those years together because of conflicting assignments. She nearly divorced him when he signed up for a second tour of duty in Vietnam just four months after the first ended. After he had been missing in action for two years, Beth had her husband declared dead and married Dirk Simon. During Sam's leap, Al, tried in vain to change his own history so he could still be married to Beth. Instead he settled for a holographic "dance" with his beloved. (MIA)

Later, when it looked as though he might pop out of existence, he told Gooshie he wanted to leave everything he had to Beth. (BRIGHT)

While we don't know the name of Al's second wife, it's speculated she's Hungarian, as Al picked up a little of the language from her (NET). She threw small appliances when she was angry (RUNAWAY), and her divorce attorney took Al for every nickel he had (SPONT).

Al's third wife, Ruthie, was Jewish and taught him all of the basics of the religion. She used to make great gefiltefish. Al has said he never knew how much family meant to him until she was gone (SHALT). Once when they were in Cleveland they had a Massage-a-Matic running for nine hours straight because there was nothing else to do (TALE).

She used the Yiddish word *mensch* (meaning "good guy") a lot, but never used it to describe Al (NUCLEAR). When they divorced, Ruthie charged Al with abuse for singing 'Volare' in his sleep (RAPED). Heiress Vanessa Foster reminded Al of Ruthie, but we don't know if it was her looks or because she was a spoiled brat, or both (SHREW).

Sharon was Al's fourth wife. She wore pink baby dolls on their honeymoon (HONEYMOON). The two were crazy about each other, but didn't know how to handle it. Sometimes Al would just grab her and kiss her (STAND). She also used to mother Al all the time, even cutting his steak when they went to dinner. This, Al says, is why he doesn't eat meat (EVIL). They also had a bitter custody battle over a dog named Chester (SPONT).

When she was suing for more alimony, Al's lawyer told him to wear a conservative suit, thinking it would help his case if he looked more boring. Sharon postponed the meeting for a few hours because her Mercedes was in the shop. Later they "examined each other's briefs and decided to call it even". (FUTURE)

Al's fifth wife was named Maxine, and she didn't wear anything in bed during their honeymoon, and flavoured her toes with mintleaves (HONEYMOON). She had a dream of roller-skating professionally – in the Roller Derby. Al recalled that as much as she tried, she always fell on her touchie. Next she tried ice skating, but was no good at that. Al says he bursts into tears when he sees a roller skate (PLAY).

They met at a tattoo parlor in Jersey City. Al has said she looks very much like Diane Frost. They used to fight all the time. (HUNT)

He has given two stories concerning the end of their relationship. One was that she ran off with a bricklayer (PLAY). The other was that he divorced her because he was 99.9% certain she was cheating on him – with a Marine. Later he found out she was innocent (HUNT). She was suing Al for more alimony on September 18, 1999 (BACK).

Al's current girlfriend is Tina, who works at Project Quantum Leap. They met in Las Vegas over a poker game. "I had a flush, and she had a pair. What a pair!" (TESS). He cheated on her quite a bit, but eventually some signs of monogamy began to show. Once Al was upset because she was gone for two weeks and he couldn't stand the "down time" (SPONT). After his consultation with Dr. Ruth, he admitted that he loved Tina (RUTH).

In no particular order, here are some of the many conquests Al claims:

A "dish" named Martha, whom he met at a Lakers game and spent the night with. Because of that, he was almost too late to help Sam fly the X-2. (PILOT)

One Saturday night his father got him out of the orphanage, and along with his girlfriend there was an extra girl. He told Al, "Son, I think it's about time . . . " (DOUBLE)

He picked up a classic car at a car show, and the photograph he showed to Sam pictured a lovely woman reclining on the hood. Al explained that she came with the car and offered to "wax his hood". (CAM)

Denise was a writer working on his life story. (HAND)

In the neighborhood where Al grew up stood a house everyone thought was haunted, and he used to take Myra Boychick there to "go bump in the night". (TROIAN)

Another childhood conquest was Shirley Mulcahey. They would go to the store for red licorice and she would get on one end and he on the other. (FREEDOM)

At MIT he had a thing for a deaf girl. She was one of the brightest women he'd ever known. "Could she read lips!" But Sam's Swiss-cheese brain somehow remembered the rest of the story – she wouldn't sleep with Al. (DANCER)

Once he dated an Egyptian girl who thought she was the reincarnation of Cleopatra. "But boy, did she have a nice asp." (CURSE)

An experience with Velvet Moreno taught him never to trust strippers. (MAYBE)

A Swedish stewardess named Oola used to tell Al bedtime stories. (PERM)

Once he dated a beauty queen – Miss Tail Gunner of 1955. And boy, Al exclaimed, did she had a "great set of turrets". (SOUTH)

Fifi "Boom-Boom" LaRue was a stripper who taught Al the art of quick draw. She had a great set of pistols, and used them in her act. (GUN)

And, in the course of duty (getting Ziggy access to classified information), he put the make on a secretary and found out that women who wear glasses have lots of energy. (RAIN)

Al's attitudes concerning women have undoubtedly been shaped by his fear of abandonment which was nurtured by both his mother and Beth leaving. Dr. Ruth postulated that he sabotages his relationships with women so he won't have to be abandoned (RUTH). Still, Al claims to have loved every woman he ever slept with – at the time he slept with them (HONEYMOON). Fidelity was highly overrated, he believed. "My relationships have all been good. It's my marriages that haven't worked out." (SHALT). On the other hand, he believes that some women get a big thrill out of watching men suffer (CHAMP).

These attitudes are reflected best in his five stages of love:
1. Denial
2. Sex
3. Acceptance
4. Divorce
5. More sex – if you're lucky (HUNT)

When Al simo–leaped with Sam, they both got a piece of each other's morality. Sam found himself leching after women, while Al was behaving like a veritable choir boy. Finally, Calavicci took over when Al made out with Suzanne Eslinga in the back of Tom Jarret's car. Later, he admitted to Sam that he had never experienced anything quite like it, and he owed it to his friend. (BACK)

"Anything to get girls" has been a long-standing Calavicci motto. After the Beatles played on *The Ed Sullivan Show*, he bought a long-haired wig (BLIND) Al also claims that he got a million hickeys from using Aqua Velva (SPONT).

Al's sexual prowess is legendary – especially in his own mind. Sex seems to be on his brain often, and he holographically leches after women. "Just call me Bigfoot," he told Sam after a discussion on Dr. Ruth's talk show about the myth that the size of a man's "love muscle" is related to his foot size. (RUTH)

Despite his so-called forward-thinking attitudes on sex, Al had a real problem using the word "breasts" in front of Dr. Ruth. Instead he used a variety of euphemisms until he ran dry and was forced to spit out the proper word. (RUTH)

Al and Sam often clashed on morals. Sam once claimed Al was a practising pervert at the age of five. (MOTHER)

Things backfired a bit when Sam leaped into Samantha Stormer. "Time has packaged my best friend as a goddess of love," Al moaned when he found himself falling in love with the physical aura of Samantha. Dr. Beeks thought perhaps Al had some repressed homosexuality, and that it would take five years of therapy before he could accept Sam as a woman. The psychiatrist taught Al that Sam is his best friend, and that love is a part of friendship. Fortunately, that staightened Al out. Good thing, too, because Al was having problems performing with Tina. (GLORIA)

Through all of his relationships, Al never fathered a child. He felt that dragging children around from assignment to assignment wasn't good for them. (MIA)

Despite Al's attitudes concerning women, he seems to believe in equal opportunities. Still, he never could decide if women's liberation was a hindrance or a help. Tina thought he was a male chauvinist pig. (LIBERATION)

Following the hard Navy line, Al has shown evidence of homophobia. He believed that homosexuals could be easily blackmailed and do not possess leadership qualities. Al changed his mind after Sam leaped into Tommy York. The change was partly due to Sam's more open-minded attitude, and partly because of the attitudes and actions of the openly gay people he observed. (HONOR)

One can assume that as a former astronaut and current naval Admiral, Al has met his share of famous people. Still, he gets very star-struck. While Sam was on the set of *Earthquake*, Al spotted Lorne Green (DISCO), and during a later leap thought he spotted Green's co-star Dan Blocker (GUN). When Sam leaped into Marilyn Monroe's driver, Al went crazy when the star went for a nude dip in her pool. Much to his credit, though, when Sam had to perform CPR on Monroe, he refrained from comment and leering (NORMA).

Al believes in the Devil, and say that his experience as a POW showed him that the Devil exists. Still, after his break with the Catholic church, he had a lot of trouble believing in God, and when Sam leaped into a Catholic priest, he refused to enter the sanctuary of the church. When Sam was shot in the head during the same leap, Al entered the sanctuary, knelt down beside the body of his friend and prayed for his life. This may have helped heal the rift. (FAITH)

Interestingly, Al is easily spooked, and tends to believe in the supernatural more than he will admit. He was antsy when in the Bermuda Triangle (SHIP) and in the tomb of Ptah-Hotep (CURSE). When Sam leaped into a parapsychologist and made Al enter a crypt, the latter got a real case of the creeps. Sam joked that there was a lovely blonde Al might like – she was rotting away in a casket that had been opened by a recent earthquake. Al jumped and exclaimed he was not into necrophilia. "At last," Sam cried, looking upward, "something sexual he's not into." (TROIAN)

When Sam leaped into a mortician Al felt like he should really sit that one out, especially after Sam declared he would have to perform an autopsy (DEAR). Even the thought of Bigfoot scared him, and Al hoped "that the hairy devil can't see holograms" (BEAST). After Sam leaped into Nigel Corrington, Al believed the eccentric artist was a vampire and took to wearing garlic and a cross. He told Sam that Nigel had all of the marks of a vampire – pale complexion, beady eyes and a lustful stare. Sam retorted that Al had just described himself (BLOOD).

A passionate environmentalist, Al decried the Queen Mary's dumping its garbage in the ocean (BRIDE) and once said Styrofoam cups came straight from Hell (STROBE). Yet he is almost never seen without a Chivello cigar in his hand.

Al is a big soul fan, having seen Aretha Franklin, James Brown and others at Chicago's Regal Theatre during its heyday (SONG). He also knows his rock and roll music, once helping Sam pick hits to play on WOF radio in Peoria (PEORIA).

Ethnic food is one of his joys. Besides Jewish treats (SHALT), Al loves menudo (ALL), crawfish gumbo (COMFORT) and chitlins (COLOR). He also loves weddings. Perhaps, he mused, because he was married five times (MACHIKO).

While Al is in good physical shape, he claims to hate calisthenics – unless they're being led by Jane Fonda. (ALL)

He likes running barefoot through sprinklers, and used to like to play "Laura" on rainy nights in front of the fire. (DEAR)

Al is also a big sports fan, enjoying both basketball and football. And, of course, he used to play baseball. He also likes fly fishing (PILOT) and classic cars (CAM). Currently he drives a modified Testarosa (PILOT, KILLIN), but his first car was a bike – a 1948 Harley Kuncklehead (REBEL).

Reflecting his life, Al's talents and skills are varied. Skilled in electronics, he helped Sam build the Imaging Chamber (CATCH) and helped Sam modify Dr. Mintz's equipment to pick up low-level battery emissions (TROIAN). Having seen *Fiddler on the Roof* five times, he helped Sam lead the Hora at a Jewish wedding (SHALT). He also taught Sam the art of the quick draw (GUN). He took fencing lessons at one time (PIANO), but probably never had piano lessons, for he admitted to Sam he couldn't play 'Chopsticks' in Chinatown (BLIND).

Al appears to Sam as a hologram. For more information on that, see HOLOGRAM, NEURO.

Other basic data: As a 2-star Rear Admiral working on PQL, he has a Top Secret clearance (NAM). Height: 172.56 cm. Weight: 70.91 kg (BACK).

After Sam leaped into Al's Place in Cokeburg, PA, he told Al the bartender his one regret was not being able to save Al's marriage. After admitting that, he leaped to Beth's house in 1959 and told her that Al was alive and would be coming home. History was changed, and now Al and Beth will celebrate their 39th wedding anniversary in the year 2000. They have had four children. (MIRROR)

Calavicci, Beth

Al's first wife. Although Al mentioned his first wife was a redhead, Beth is definitely a brunette. Did Al merely indulge in a little wishful thinking? Only her hairdresser knows for sure. Beth loves calla lilies, Mexican food and Ray Charles singing 'Georgia'. She also seems to be a fan of the Supremes, especially the song 'Someday'. Al declares that Beth was the only woman he ever truly loved. She was upset because he didn't want children because he thought it was unfair to drag them from assignment to assignment. She, on the other hand, felt Al didn't understand what children would have done for her while he was gone. During the eight years they were married, they only spent two together. The rest were spent on separate assignments. Beth nearly divorced Al when he took off for a second tour of duty to Vietnam four months after the first ended. She didn't feel it was proper to divorce a man going off to war, and, after Al was shot down, she wore an M.I.A. bracelet engraved with his name. She was working double shifts as a nurse in the burn ward at Balboa Naval Hospital when, in March 1969, she lost a young Marine that she thought was going to beat the odds and live. She apparently gave up hope on Al at about the same time, for on April 1 she met Dirk Simon, and despite Al's trying to change history (through Sam trying to keep Beth away from Dirk), the pair kept running into each other. They finally married in June of that year. (MIA)

Sam got to change history for Beth and Al after he leaped into Al's place in Cokeburg, PA. When he confessed to Al the bartender his regrets about not saving Al's marriage, he leaped to Beth's house and told her Al was coming home. Subsequently, they had four children and will celebrate their 39th anniversary in the year 2000. (MIRROR)

Calavicci, Trudy

Al's younger sister was born retarded, possibly with Down's Syndrome. Of course they didn't use that term in those days. It was simply retarded. Al loved his sister very much, and considers the pressure of raising her was part of the reason their mother ran off with an encyclopedia salesman. Her IQ was lower than that of Jimmy LaMotta. When Al was old enough to get out of the orphanage, he went after Trudy and found she had died of pheumonia at the age of 16. To this day he is distressed over her death. (JIMMY)

Calla Lilies

Beth's favorite flower. Al told Sam to woo her with them. Moe Stein also brought calla lilies home to his wife whenever he came home from the road.

Calloway, Jason

Michael Blake's perennial yes-man. (MIRACLE)

Camille

One of the deadliest hurricanes ever, it hit the coast of the Gulf of Mexico with winds up to 190 mph. Over 360 people were killed, and Sam was trying to bring that number down by at least one. (HURRICANE)

Camp Chipmunk

The Rickett family spent six months trying to get reservations at this campground for the Fourth of July holiday. (RUNAWAY)

Captain Z-RO

An early 1950s sci-fi series about a scientist who had invented a rocket ship that could also travel in time. Sam was watching this program at Al's Place when Ziggy (a miner who looked just like Moe Stein/Captain Galaxy) walked in. (MIRROR)

Carla

Cheerleader for the Jaguars. She had the hots for quarterback Eddie Vega/Sam. (ALL)

Castro, Fidel

When Sam was a firefighter rescuing a kitten 1957, Al told him he was there to stop Castro from taking power. Al's plan was to get Sam to change a major world event, thereby ensuring funding for the Project. (HONEY-MOON)

Chadwick, Brian

Kevin Wentworth's defense attorney. (RAPED)

Chain, the

A group of cadets at Prescott Naval Academy who believed they were honoring an "ideal Navy". Mainly, they were violent gay-bashers. Of the five involved in the murder of Phillip Ashcroft in the original history, only Ronnie Chambers was convicted. (HONOR)

Chambers, Ronnie, Cadet Lt. Comdr.

A cadet on the track team at Prescott Naval Academy with Tommy York, and ringleader of a group known as the Chain. (HONOR)

Chapman, Joanna

In 1979 she ran one of the best modern jazz dance groups in the nation. Sam convinced her to give a young deaf dancer named Diana Quina a shot. (DANCER)

Charlmont State Hospital

Sam was taken to this institution by Max Stoddard's family, who were having the old man committed. (BRIGHT)

Chase, Davey

A boy from Cheyenne, Wyoming who wrote to Captain Galaxy and asked if he and Superman got into a fight, who would win. (FUTURE)

Chatham, Nurse

Sometimes she seemed like the only truly compassionate person on the staff at Havenwell Hospital. Acting on her own, she gave Sam the does of shock treatment to get him out and Beederman back. (SHOCK)

Checker, Chubby

He visited WOF radio in Peoria in 1959 when Sam was there as a DJ. Sam showed him how to do the Twist, and convinced Rachel Porter to play the record. (PEORIA)

Cheree

Cheree and her friends had formed a Supremes-style singing group called The Dovetts. Cheree/Sam had to keep one of the members, Lynelle Walters, from signing her life away to a sleazy promoter named Bobby Lee. (SONG)

"Cherry Buster"

Tom Jarret's 1941 Oldsmobile convertible. (BACK)

Chippendales Dancers

Sam leaped into one of these male striptease artists in 1979. (DANCER)

Chloe

This seemingly ditzy girl worked at Frank Bianca's salon in Beverly Hills. She hired Detective Ward to kill Phil Hartman, who had been supplying her drugs to sell to customers at the salon. (WAVE)

Chopin

Pianist Andrew Ross's seeing-eye dog. (BLIND)

Chopsticks

Before he remembered he could play the piano, Sam found himself in the position of having to play an encore for virtuoso Andrew Ross. The best he could come up with was this song. Fortunately for him, the audience thought it was rather witty. (BLIND)

Chu Hoi

Military slang for a Vietcong guerrilla who had joined the other side. The young lady who was leading Tom's S.E.A.L. unit to a POW rescue was actually leading them into an ambush. (NAM)

Claggett Brothers

They used to control Coffin, Arizona until Tyler Means and Pat Knight rode in and cleaned up the town. (GUN)

Clapper

Word on the street was "dropper" named Clapper "offed" Phil Grimsley. Al wondered if there wasn't a cure for that. (SEYMOUR)

Claridge, Julian

A writer of Gothic romances who died in 1968, just as violently as his ancestors. He drowned in the lake on the Claridge estate as his wife was painting a picture of him. Julian was sitting in a rowboat, and he got bored and began to clown around, and fell over. Despite his being a superb swimmer, he never came to the surface.

The Claridge family history is quite checkered. In 1840 Nathaniel (who died eight years later) caught his wife Priscilla in the attic with the butler *in flagrante*. He drowned them both. Their bodies, along with that of Julian, surfaced during the aftershock of an earthquake. All were remarkably well preserved due to the extreme cold at the bottom of the lake. (TROIAN)

Claridge, Troian Giovanni

She illustrated her husband Julian's Gothic romance novels. Trioan had just returned to Lakeview, California, three years after the death of her husband. She claims to have heard his voice the night they gave up searching for his body, and began hearing it again three years later. (TROIAN)

Claudia

Victor Drake's companion accompanied her lover to Nigel Corrington's castle for the Blood Moon ceremony. She wanted to bathe in Nigel's power, and bore her fangs and attempted to bite Sam. Her "fangs" turned out to be fancy bridgework. (BLOOD)

Cleary's Bookstore

Sam found himself "standing in" for Dr. Ruth Westheimer's autograph session here. (RUTH)

Clover Bend, Texas

Billy Beaumont's home town. Sam made it rain there, despite the odds that it wouldn't for months. (RAIN)

Clyde

Sam leaped into this man just as he was being inducted into the Ku Klux Klan. Apparently Clyde didn't hold to the KKK ideals, but joined to appease his father-in-law, Tom. Clyde felt that all men were equal, and was trying to teach his son Cody that lesson. His wife Lillian called the Klan her daddy's "hunting club". (JUSTICE)

Cobras

A motorcycle gang roaming the country circa 1958. Sam found himself part of that gang in September of that year. (REBEL)

Cockfight

Southern prison slang for a fight to the death between two prisoners. Sam used it as a cover for his prison break with Jasper Boone. (UNCHAINED)

Cocoa Puffs

Jimmy LaMotta's favorite breakfast cereal. (JIMMY)

Cocono Club

Known as The Cocono in the Poconos, this is where Parker and MacKay were bombing when Sam leaped into Davey Parker. (STAND)

Cody, Clarence "Kid

An out-of shape fighter whose best days were behind him. In fact, Cody hadn't won a straight fight in a year. Cody's contract had been inherited by a group of nuns, and they were expecting him to win his next fight so they could have the funds to build a chapel. (HAND)

Coffin, Arizona

In 1957 this town was celebrating its centennial, and Tyler Means was re-creating his legendary gun battle with the Claggett Brothers daily. The town started as a robbers' hangout, and then took off when silver was discovered in the mid-1870s. The Claggett Brothers controlled the town, and the story went that Tyler Means and his partner rode in and cleaned up the town. Tyler settled there. (GUN)

Cokeburg, Pennsylvania

Coal-mining town where Al's Place was located. (MIRROR)

66

Cole, Chance Terrance

He was serving the second year of what should have been a nine-month prison term at the Tallawaga County Prison when he decided to break out with Jasper Boone. (UN-CHAINED)

Cole, Margaret

Lawyer Reed Dalton's wife. After an indictment, Reed took their baby, Christina, changed his last name to Dalton, and left. He told everyone that his wife had died in childbirth. (MAYBE)

Collins, Detective, Max

San Francisco police officer investigating a series of killings in Chinatown. (EYES)

Collins, Gloria

Samantha Stormer's roommate worked with her in the steno pool at National Motors. She believed she was going to marry Buddy Wright, a married executive at the company. She would have committed suicide over him had Sam not talked her out of it. Gloria eventually married a man named Parker whom she met on a blind double date set up by Samantha's mother. (GLORIA)

Collins, Mr.

Superintendent of the mine in Cokeburg, PA. He was dead set against an attempt to rescue Tonchi and Pete. (MIRROR)

Constantine, Shirley

Frank LaMotta's secretary at the Oakland Docks. He was on the verge of having an affair with her, and Ziggy said he would leave Connie for her if Sam didn't do something about it. She was 25 years old, had graduated from Sawyer Secretarial School, and was a high school gymnastics champion. (EVIL)

Conway, Dr. Dale

An archaeology professor from Kansas State University on the dig for Ptah-Hotep in Egypt in 1957. Sam had done a thesis on Conway and the ancient pharaoh, and was thrilled to have leaped into him at the tomb site. (CURSE)

Cooley

A guard at Tallawaga County Prison who was behind a string of robberies falsely attributed to one of the prisoners. (UNCHAINED)

Coolidge, Vernon

Ran the gas station in Clover Bend, Texas. (RAIN)

Cooper, "Coop" and Wendy

Husband-and-wife pilot-stewardess team that flew a corporate jet for Grant Cutter's father. Cooper had located and sunk seven U-boats in the Bermuda Triangle during the Second World War, and began having flashbacks about a trip where he lost his squadron. (SHIP)

Corfu

When Sam and Vanessa Foster finally hit land, she thought they'd landed here. Not only was she wrong, but the island on which they landed was uninhabited, and would be for another nine years. (SHREW)

Corrington, Lord Nigel

London's most eccentric and expensive artist inhabits the same castle in which his family has lived for five generations. Although he just shocked the art world by marrying a homeless girl named Alexandra Hill, no one at all seems to take notice of Lord Nigel's rather unconventional lifestyle. In fact, living like a vampire may just be a marketing ploy, as Sam pointed out to a rather spooked Al. Of course, Sam was a bit spooked himself to awaken in a coffin at sunset, greeted by a lithe young lady and a creepy servant making cryptic remarks to livestock. Naturally there were no mirrors in the castle, so Sam found it rather annoying that he couldn't sneak a look at his reflection. Al informed Sam that he looked just like the man in a painting in the study, which was supposed to be one of Nigel's ancestors. Was Nigel what he claimed to be? Sam finally found a silver serving tray and saw no reflection. (BLOOD)

Cory

Chimp #63 at Cape Canaveral, in contention to be one of the first chimps in space. She has a crush on Bob, the "chimp next door" cage-wise. She and Bobo ended up having a baby together, but well after Sam had leaped out. (WRONG)

Casta, Raul

Along with Jesus Ortega, he was convicted and sentenced to death for the murder of Father Vincent Torelli. Sam proved Costa's innocence, and Raul is now living with his daughter in Florida. (LAST)

Cotter, Colbert, Captain

This powerful man ran the town of Twelve Oaks, LA. He and Leonard Dancey's dad were partners for a long time, so the Captain gave his legal business to Leonard. (HELP)

Cotter, Sadie

Married to Captain Cotter. She took Lila Barry in when she was fourteen. Lila had been living in a bayou, and she and her mother had buried seven brothers and sisters there. Sadie was compassionate, and felt sorry for the girl. Her son Houston took a liking to Lila also, raping her shortly after she arrived. Lila loved Houston, and he her, but he couldn't marry her. Sadie gave Lila enough money to go away and start a new life, but Houston arrived just as Lila was leaving and a fight broke out. Sadie remembered that she picked up the gun and it went off, but she doesn't remember that Houston was killed. (HELP)

Cougar

The type of fighter plane Al flew as an Ensign. (LISA)

Cougars

The name of the Elk Ridge basketball team. Sam played on that team in 1969. (HOME)

70

Covington, Olivia Barrett

Sam's great-grandmother was a southern belle before the Civil War. After her husband Daniel died, she tended to the plantation and ran a stop on the Underground Railroad. (STATES)

Crane, Mason

This psychiatrist had been seeing both the deceased Janice DeCaro and her husband Peter. Mason was one of the most respected psychiatrists in Los Angeles, where he practiced until 1983. After that he moved to Chicago, where he presumably retired – or so it went in the original history. Crane claimed to have a gift of knowing when people are telling the truth or not, and attempted to help Sam sort out a series of bad dreams and flashbacks. In reality, he was setting up Sam's murder. (DREAMS)

Cranston's Roller Palace

Captain Galaxy and Future Boy did a personal appearance there. (FUTURE)

Crockett, Billie Jean

She was sixteen and VERY pregnant when Sam leaped in to help her keep her baby instead of giving it up for adoption, a decision she ended up regretting for the rest of her life. Although she had been in full labor, Sam's leap somehow arrested it, and he had 36 hours to change Billie Jean's life for the better. Sam reunited the girl with her estranged father, who helped to take care of the baby. (8½)

Crockett, Bob

Billie Jean's father was a foreman at Kip Petroleum. He didn't know who the father of her child was and refused to have anything to do with the baby. When Sam had a talk with him it may have softened his heart, because he ended up marrying his high school sweetheart Dotty Billings and the two of them helped Billie Jean with the baby. (8½)

Crosnoff, Doc

The Beckett family lawyer. Sam actually described him as his dad's attorney. When Sam and Al simo-leaped, Al ended up with the handlink and the only way out of the Imaging Chamber, save a backdoor override code that could be used from the outside console. Al mailed a packet containing a letter to Crosnoff, a letter to Gooshie with the code, and $100 for the attorney's trouble, instructing that the letter to Gooshie must arrive on September 18, 1999. Indeed, the programmer remarked that the packet arrived 54 years, 7 months and 6 days after Al mailed it. (BACK)

Crown Electric

Elvis Presley worked there as a truck driver before he embarked on his singing career. (MEMPHIS)

Cuban Missile Crisis

Sam found himself smack in the middle of this bit of history, and only 200 miles from Cuba, selling fallout shelters. (NUCLEAR)

'Cuanda Le Gusta'

When Sam found himself in the Miss Deep South beauty pageant, he learned that his "talent" was to dress up as Carmen Miranda and dance to this song (SOUTH). Sam told Al he didn't know the song, but he had heard it at least once, as Victor Panzini. The act that performed before the Panzinis was Carmendita and Her Friends, a "Brazilian" lady who shimmied to the song with a group of dogs in tow. (NET)

Curse of Ptah-Hotep

Sam red the hieroglyphics in Ptah-Hotep's tomb as saying, "As for anyone who will disturb the tome of King Ptah-Hotep, death will swallow him up." It apparently happened to Mustafa el Rassul. (CURSE)

Cutrell, Mrs.

The baby-sitter Maggie Spontini hired to stay with Jamie while she went to the custody hearing. (SPONT)

Cutter, Grant & Michelle

Grant was heir to a huge petroleum company, and he and his wife Michelle (née Temple) were on their honeymoon to Bermuda. At first, Grant did not understand how seriously ill his wife was when she got acute appendicitis. After her appendix burst, Sam improvised an IV from a douche bag, which saved her life. (SHIP)

D

Dalton, Christie

The infant daughter of Reed Dalton, Sam and Bunny O'Hare saw that she got back to her natural mother. (MAYBE)

Dalton, Reed

A powerful Texas lawyer whom everyone believed to be a widower. While he told everyone his wife had died in childbirth, his "companion" Bunny O'Hare found the truth and attempted to get the child back to her natural mother. Reed's real last name is Cole, and he left New Mexico after milking millions from investors in a real-estate scam and being disbarred. He took his baby daughter along. (MAYBE)

Dancey, Leonard

Defense attorney for Lila Barry, a black woman accused of murdering the son of her white employer. (HELP)

Dancey, Sugie

Leonard's social-climbing wife. She was absolutely appalled when her husband tried to prove Lila (whom she called a "whore") innocent of murder. Everything worked out okay in the end, though. After Sam won the trial, he got an offer from a large law firm in Baton Rouge, and it included a country club membership. (HELP)

Danner, Hilla

A young German immigrant who apparently committed suicide on her 19th birthday – November 9, 1957. Her father had died in North Africa, and the rest of her family perished in the fire-bombing of Dresden. She spent the rest of the war in a displaced persons' camp, and fought off a lot of men. She had fallen in love with Greg Truesdale, son of the owner of Truesdale Lodge. He had made her pregnant, but according to her diary she had met someone else. After much digging by Sam, it was revealed that Greg was actually the someone else, and the first person she had been in love with was Stephanie, a co-worker who was hoping to become a professional photographer. She thought that after the war she could never know what love was with a man – until she met Greg. She and Stephanie had an argument when she tried to explain her feelings, and Stephanie lashed out and hit her in the head with the spiked heel of her shoe. (DEAR)

Dante, Coach

Coached the Jaguars, where Sam found himself as quarterback. In all of his 32 years of coaching, he'd never seen a play as ugly as the one Sam executed when he leaped in.

But since it resulted in a touchdown, it was fine with him. (ALL)

Davies, Jerry

Chi Kappa Delta pledge who was participating in a chicken race as a hazing ritual. After the Midnight Marauder/Sam stopped the race, Jerry decided not to join the fraternity. (RETURN)

Davis, Cissy

Archie Necaise's girlfriend was a nurse and Red Cross worker who helped evacuate people from the path of hurricane Camille. In the original history she got killed at her house when debris smashed through the window. After Sam kept her away from her house, the projection changed and she was going to be killed at Unabelles, the inn where many of the evacuees were housed. Sam arrived at the inn with enough time left to prevent her death at the hands of Archie's ex-girlfriend. After the storm passed, Sam convinced Cissy to go back to school and become a psychotherapist. (HURRICANE)

Davis, Eddie

A sleazy pool shark who held the marker on Violet Walters' blues club. Charlie "Black Magic" Walters/Sam had to beat Davis in a match in order for Violet to keep the club. (POOL)

Dawson, Maggie

Famous photojournalist who joined Tom Beckett's Bravo S.E.A.L. unit on a mission. She told Sam she would give her soul for a Pulitzer. Maggie was tough, having been through three wars and five insurrections, night patrol with the Marines, in a tank with the Israelis and a bombing raid over Hai Phong. Her security clearance was signed by Westmoreland himself. She "persuaded" Sam to convince Tom that there was something magic about her and that she should accompany them on Operation Lazarus the next day. Partly because of her presence, Sam saved Tom, but Maggie tripped over a booby trap and died. She had just photographed a group of American POWs being led through the jungle. As she expired, she saw Al, and handed Sam the camera, uttering the word "Pulitzer". The pictures showed one of the POWS was Al. (NAM)

DeCaro, Janice

When Sam leaped into Detective Jack Stone, he discovered her horribly mutilated body, which in turn triggered a series of flashbacks. (DREAMS)

DeCaro, P. J.

Peter and Janice De'Caro's son. He went into shock upon seeing his mother's body, and would not utter a word. Sam finally coaxed a clue out of him – a drawing of a pair of gloves. The gloves belonged to D. Mason Crane. (DREAMS)

DeCaro, Peter

After his wife Janice was found murdered, Sam discovered Peter with a gun to his head, calmly saying he had to talk to Janice. Sam saved his life, but in the original history Peter got the chair for killing Sam/Jack Stone. (DREAMS)

DeGorio, Carlo

The owner of the Las Vegas Golden Sand Hotel was used to getting what he wanted, even if it meant feeding someone to the coyotes in the desert. He spotted Frankie Washarski in the Poconos and invited Parker and MacKay out – as long as she was part of the act. In the original history, he bumped off Mack MacKay because he was getting between him and Frankie, but after Sam explained that Mack and Frankie were engaged, DeGorio offered to pay for their wedding. (STAND)

DeGuerra, Ruben

He owned the home Celia and Chuey Martinez lived in along with half a dozen or so other houses he rented at exorbitant rates to people who couldn't complain – such as Celia, who was an illegal immigrant. (ALL)

DeNardo, Joey

Sam leaped into this man as he was playing a piano bar called The Roadside Rendezvous in Tullarosa, New Mexico under the name of Chuck Tanner. Joey had witnessed a Mafia hit and had changed his name and left to protect his fiancée Lorraine. Lorraine tracked him down, and over the next 24 hours they fled someone who was trying to kill them. That someone turned out to be Nick Bellini, a childhood friend who had committed the murder Joey witnessed. Lorraine and Joey got married and ended up in Hawaii, performing nightly at the "Tiki Tiki in Wakikiki". (PIANO)

Decca Records

Sam convinced the head of the company to listen to The Dovettes sing, hoping the label would sign the group to a contract. (SONG)

Deever, Joe

Cissy Davis' ex-boyfriend came to Unabelle's to ride out hurricane Camille with his sister and her kids. He was insanely jealous with a hot temper, but Cissy trusted him because they grew up together and he had never touched her the entire time they dated. He had been the last person to see Cissy alive in the original history. (HURRICANE)

Deke's Dragon

The name of Colonel Grimwald's helicopter. (NAM)

Demons and Dragons

Like many high school kids in 1981, Kevin Bruckner and his friends were Demons and Dragons freaks. Al hates that game. (MOTHER)

Despartes, Chester

He owned the biggest gas station in Shreveport, and sent a group of Shriners over to Gilbert LaBonte's "house", telling them it was the place to have a good time while in New Orleans, (COMFORT)

79

Devil's Backbone

When Emma Rickett left her family on July 4, 1966 she had just gone off to think things over, but slipped and fell over a ridge at this landmark. Skeletal remains presumed to be hers were found at is base in 1993. (RUNAWAY)

Dick

Samantha Stormer/Sam found he had a blind date with this man that had been set up by Samantha's mother. Dick and his buddy Porter worked for a washer company, selling 786 sizes made out of 31 different materials. When Sam couldn't take his advances any more and hit him, he called Samantha a feisty little wench. (GLORIA)

Dillon

The Brando-esque leader of the Cobras, a motorcycle gang that roamed the country circa 1958. He was a tough guy, and was bitter over his experiences fighting in Korea. He used and abused others to stay on top, and if Sam hadn't come along he would have murdered Becky, the girl who rode with the gang. Instead, he got some time in jail. (REBEL)

Dingles, The

King Thunder was known by this name when they first toured America in the 1950s. (ROCK)

Disco

Worse than anything imaginable for Sam. He would rather die. (DISCO)

Disco Inferno

Sam was a stunt man on this motion picture. Al recalled having seen it on cable. He gave it the thumbs down. (DISCO)

Dixie

Kid Cody's lover. She was a topless dancer by profession. They were saving all of their money in the hopes of eventually scraping $20,000 together so they could open a donut shop. When Sam asked her to streak during the championship fight so he would have a chance to win, she felt degraded. Sam explained that being a topless dancer is a profession just like any other, and she shouldn't feel ashamed, but also that he believed her streak was his only hope of winning he fight. Sam had also instructed Dixie (against her better judgment) to bet their entire life-savings on the Ali-Foreman fight. Of course, Sam knew the outcome, so the bet was safe. They eventually retired to their donut shop on their share of the winnings. (HAND)

Doobs, Hugh Cmdr. (US Navy)

Bingo's defense attorney. (LISA)

Dorleac, Gina

After she found out she was pregnant, Gina left her abusive husband in Lake Charles and sought refuge with her cousin, Marsha, a brothel madam in New Orleans. Marsha let Gina stay, but refused to tell the house proprietor, Gilbert LaBonte, that she wasn't a "working girl" for fear they would both be turned out. After Gilbert/Sam helped Gina stand up to her husband, she and Marsha went to Atlanta and she gave birth to a boy named Gilbert. (COMFORT)

Dorleac, Jake

He showed up at the LaBonte house claiming to be looking for a runaway from his girls' finishing school. In reality, he was looking for his wife of two years, Gina. She had runaway because he was abusive, and he tried to take her from the house by force, but was stopped by Sam. Sam eventually managed to set up a compromising photography in which Dorleac was seen in an embrace with a hooker. Dorleac was so embarrassed about the possibility of that picture appearing in the paper that he never went back to Lake Charles. His hot temper got him into so much trouble that he ended up in a mental hospital. (COMFORT)

Downey, Laura, Captain (Salvation Army)

When Michael Blake made plans to demolish the 4th Street Mission, Captain Downey fought back. After Blake refused to answer her calls, she took a brass band up to his penthouse apartment and definitely got his attention. In fact, the got married and Blake put the mission on the first floor of Blake Plaza. (MIRACLE)

Dovettes, The

A Supremes-type singing group in Chicago, circa 1963. The three teenagers who made up the group were Lynelle Walters and her friends' Cheree and Paula. (SONG)

Drake, Victor

He was honored by Nigel Corrington's invitation to take part in the Blood Moon ritual, and it was obvious he took vampire lore seriously. Seriously enough to kill Lord Corrington's dog Vlad in an apparent thirst for blood. After Sam called off the ceremony, he drugged Sam and Corrington's wife Alexandra, and made preparations to sacrifice the young lady at the top of Nigel's castle while a lightning storm raged overhead. As Sam lunged for Drake, lightning struck the upraised dagger, the shock hurtling Victor to his death below. (BLOOD)

Duck and Cover

As Kimberley and Stevie Ellroy watched this film on TV, Sam remarked to Al that he was concerned it would give them the idea that they could survive a nuclear blast. Al said that it gave the kids a sense of control, so in that respect it was good for them. (NUCLEAR)

Dumont, Phillip

Sam leaped into this sailor on June 3, 1954, on the day of his ex-wife's wedding. Phillip was still in love with Catherine Farlington, and although she wouldn't admit it, she still loved him. But she was bitter that he had left three years before and never returned. In reality, he was marooned at sea for three years when his mainsail broke and he used the jib to row to Bora Bora. Catherine's father, Weathers Farlington IV, convinced her that Phillip was dead and had the marriage annulled. He didn't like Phillip because he refused to enter the family business. Sam eventually succeeded in getting Kate and Phillip back together. (BRIDE)

Duncan, Connie

Miss Corn Muffin in the Miss Deep South contest hailed from Buford City and wanted to be in the movies, but she wasn't going to finish the contest because pageant photographer Clint Beaumont took her up to his room for a clandestine photo session. A month later, her picture would turn up in a calendar – the kind you see in your better muffler shops around the country. She was so embarrassed that she left the pageant and was never heard from again. Darlene Monty/Sam was her roommate at the pageant and helped her get out of the clutches of the sleazy photographer. After the pageant she went home and started a community theatre, and now lives a good life. (SOUTH)

E

Earthquake

Chad Stone/Sam was a stunt man on this film, and Al went nuts over seeing "Ben Cartwright" (Lorne Greene) on the set. (DISCO)

Edwards Air Force Base

Tom Stratton/Sam was stationed at this base where the first supersonic test flights took place. (PILOT)

Edwards, Harlan

Manager of the Galveston Mustangs baseball team. (BALL)

Edward, Jake

A very shady fight promoter in California. He paid off a number of fighters, including Kid Cody/Sam, to take dives when he told them to. Sam got out from under him by betting everything on the Ali-Foreman fight in 1974 and winning a bundle. (HAND)

85

Effie

A young girl who worked at Dotty Billings' beauty salon, doing odd jobs. She was very scared when Billie Jean Crockett went into labor because her own sister bled to death in her mother's arms at the age of 17 due to complications resulting from childbirth. (8½)

Eisenberg, Jani

Investigative reporter at KDNM-TV, Destiny, New Mexico. She had been a hot-shot journalist in Chicago, but was forced to move because of her asthma. She and Roberto Gutierrez/Sam were pursuing a story about a chemical company testing illegal weapons. (ROBERTO)

el Rassul, Mustaffah, Dr.

Head of the Department of Antiquities at Luxor Museum, a partner in the dig for Ptah-Hotep. In the end, el Rassul attempted to take the spoils of the dig for himself, but was foiled, apparently by the Curse of Ptah-Hotep. (CURSE)

Elaine

A performer working the Blue Mamba club with Harry Spontini in 1974. She'd worked for months to get the two of them booked together, and was upset to think that Harry still loved his wife who had left three years before. (SPONT)

Elesee, Donna

Is she or isn't she married to Sam? Only God or Time or Whoever knows. In the history as Sam remembered it when he met her as a student in Lawrence College in 1972, Donna was just turning 30 and leaving the Starbright Project when they first met around 1982. The wedding was on the 5th of June at Old Mission Chapel, and Sam remembers it didn't happen. Al told Sam she didn't show up for the wedding, and Sam then remembered it had something to do with her father. He abandoned her when she was eight and had no more contact with her. Donna was so upset she blocked out her dad's name, Wojohowitz. She left another man at the altar before Sam. Sam arranged for Donna to meet him at the Watergate Hotel the morning he shipped out to Vietnam. Al gave no clue that Sam may have changed history, in fact he speculated that maybe she married the first guy after all. (CROSSED)

When Sam and Al changed places and he ended up back at the Project, all of his memories came flooding back and Donna was there – as his wife. Donna explained to Sam that she begged Al not to tell him he was married, for she felt he couldn't act freely with that knowledge. When Sam asked if he did anything to hurt her, her reply was no. When Sam had to leap again in order to save Al, she begged him not to go, but realized in the end she had to let Sam go. (BACK)

Elias, B. T.

Warden at Tallawaga County Prison. (UNCHAINED)

Ellis, Mr. and Mrs.

The mayor of Oak Creek, OH and his wife. Machiko MacKenzie made a grave social blunder by "complimenting" them on how fat they were. (MACHIKO)

Ellroy, Eddie

A student at Oklahoma State, he was trying to earn enough money to finish school by selling bomb shelters for his brother Mac when Sam leaped into him. Eddie had wrecked his knee and lost a basketball scholarship. Sam was there to keep the Ellroys' neighbor, Burt Rosencranz, from getting shot and killed while trying to get into the family's bomb shelter. After the crisis passed, Sam suggested to Mac that his business could easily be converted to building swimming pools. Eddie graduated from college and the two of them started the largest pool-building company on south Florida. (NUCLEAR)

Ellroy, Ellen Louise

Marty's first wife had two kids called Mary and Martin (Jr.). their dog, Tinkerbell, was a pedigreed greyhound Marty bought for an investment. Ellen worked at a beauty shop, and one of her customers was Rachel, Marty's other wife. (TALE)

Ellroy, Gina

Marty's third wife. She and her two children arrived just after Marty's other two wives left him. (TALE)

Ellroy, Jessica

Marty and Rachel's daughter was young enough to see Sam and Al, and initially distrusted them as much as she did her father. She tried to run away from the family, but Al talked her into staying. (TALE)

Ellroy, Josh

Marty has taught his son by Rachel the fine art of stealing from the maids' carts at the hotel. When Sam tried to have a heart-to-heart conversation with the boy, Josh offered him what little money he had, saying that whenever they had such a conversation Marty always hit on him for cash. (TALE)

Ellroy, Kate

Mac's wife was very concerned about the daily air raid drills her family was going through, and what impact they might have on the kids. She was honestly scared about the possibility of a nuclear war. (NUCLEAR)

Ellroy, Kimberly

Mac and Kate's daughter. (NUCLEAR)

Ellroy, Mac

A Florida man who built fallout shelters, but he hadn't sold one in two years. When the Cuban Missile Crisis hit, he hoped to cash in by selling shelters, as they lived so close, missile-wise, to Cuba. In the original history he was convicted for killing his neighbor, Burt Rosencranz, as he tried to break into their fallout shelter. Mac lost his family, the home, everything. As the crisis unfolded, it turned out his son Stevie had shot Burt, but Mac took the blame. Sam averted the family crisis, and the missile crisis passed. Sam suggested they build fun instead of fear and the brothers built the largest swimming pool company in South Florida. (NUCLEAR)

Ellroy, Martin (Marty)

Sam found himself in a sticky situation when he leaped into this travelling salesman for Best Sale Brushes. Not only did he gamble heavily, but he had two families – one in Brooklyn and one in Pompano Beach. (TALE)

Ellroy, Martin Jr.

Marty's oldest boy handicapped the dog races for his dad. In appreciation, Marty brought him a shoe horn from the Fiesta Hotel. (TALE)

Ellroy, Mary

Marty's daughter by Ellen. Marty's gift for her was a shower cap. (TALE)

Ellroy, Rachel Thelma

Marty's second wife lived in Brooklyn and worked at the Long Island Turf Club. The family drove down to Pompano Beach in their station wagon to see Marty. (TALE)

Ellroy, Stevie

Mac and Kate's son was scared of a nuclear attack from Cuba, and his father was only fueling that fear by hammering home that they only lived 200 miles from the island nation. During a drill, the boy was so scared he thought a neighbor was actually an enemy soldier, and Sam stopped him from shooting by telling him to duck and cover, as he had been taught on TV. (NUCLEAR)

Ellroy Super Deluxe Shelter

"Survive in Style". That was the Ellroys' motto, and they designed a fallout shelter designed to take people right through the 60s. The shelters sold for $3,000 apiece. (NUCLEAR)

Eloch

Beverly Hills pharmacist Phil Hartman was supplying drugs to this company, and when he quit doing so, they killed him. Eloch was an anagram of Chloe, an employee at Frank Bianca's salon. She was selling the drugs to Frank's customers. (PERM)

Eslinga, Suzanne

She had been engaged to Tom Jarret before the war, but gave him up for dead after seeing an Ernie Pyle column that carried what appeared to be news of his demise. She cried her eyes out for two years, then waited another year and a half before saying yes to Clifford. Tom returned home days before the wedding. (BACK)

Engramic Standard

When Tom Stratton/Sam complained that he had forgotten how to fly, his friend Bird Dog cooked up a story for Drs. Burger and Ernst that flying at speeds greater than Mach 2 caused memory loss. The pair believed the practical joke, and cooked up a test: the Burger/Ernst (or Ernst Burger) Engramic Standard. Sam suggested it was sort of like Trivial Pursuit, a game that wouldn't be invented for another 30 years or so. He was to take the test before the flight, and again later to see if there was really memory loss. They asked some intriguing questions like what was the coldest you have ever been, who was your second-best friend in college, and where were you when you first made love? Some of the questions and Sam's answers:

Q: Date of Birth?

A: August 8, 1953.

Q: What had the most positive effect on me in high school?

A: Mini skirts.

Q: What had the most negative effect on me in high school?

A: Pantyhose.

Q: When feeling lonely, I . . . ?

A: Rent a video and microwave some popcorn.

Other answers concerned pet rocks, waterbeds, and being expelled from college for streaking.

The doctors realized the answers were given from the point of view of a man from the future, and chalked it all up to a practical joke. (PILOT)

Ernst, Dr. "Weird Ernie"

One of the officers in charge of the supersonic flight program at Edwards AFB. A metal plate in his head kept him grounded – as in, unable to fly. (PILOT)

Evilatita, Evita

A "performer" Al recalls seeing in Tijuana. She would lay on her back and play "oldies with her toesies", then lean over and play modern music with her . . . Anyway, her big finish was singing the National Anthem in 40 languages. (BLIND)

F

4th Street Mission

This Salvation Army mission had been serving lower Manhattan for over 47 years when Michael Blake purchased the property for Blake Plaza. The mission eventually went on the first floor of the skyscraper. (MIRACLE)

Fang, Dr. Laszlo

Author of the book *How to Spot a Vampire*. (BLOOD)

Farlington, Jennifer Elizabeth

Eleven-year-old sister of Catherine Farlington. Wise beyond her years, she realized that Catherine and Phillip Dumont/Sam were truly in love, and engineered their reconciliation. She also gave Vincent Loggia the moniker "Vinny the Viper". After Phillip told Jennifer his tale about being lost at sea, she wrote it as a murder mystery and it was a runaway best-seller. In fact, it kept the family fortunes afloat until the cruise business picked up in the 1970s. (BRIDE)

Farlington, Catherine

Vassar-educated heir to Farlington Nautical, she was married to Phillip Dumont, who wanted no part in the family business. Phillip sailed off to think one day, and three years later she got a note from Bora Bora saying he'd been swept away. Her father Weathers convinced Kate to have Phillip declared dead, and then mobster Vincent Loggia offered to marry Catherine and buy out Farlington Nautical. She couldn't admit she didn't love Vincent, and felt it her family duty to marry him. She backed out of the ceremony at the last minute. (BRIDE)

Farlington, Weathers IV

His company, Farlington Nautical, was in financial trouble, and his daughter Catherine was going to marry Vincent Loggia, who, in turn, had offered to buy out the company. He demonstrated his boxing skills twice, once in knocking Sam to the ground, and again in knocking out Vincent after Catherine backed out of the wedding. He was the Harvard middleweight champion in 1919. (BRIDE)

'Fate's Wide Wheel'

Hit song written by Tonic of King Thunder. Part of the lyrics went:
 "As I travel in space and time
 I want to stay, I want to go
 You can see my face – but it's not mine
 What you can't see you'll never know."
 When asked about those lyrics, Sam explained that we all live our lives behind masks, but the real point of living

is to break through those masks so we can really communicate. (ROCK)

Felcher, Rev.

The pastor where the MacKenzie family attended church. When he and his wife drove Henry and Lenore MacKenzie home, they spotted Machiko doing chores in the heat the Japanese way – topless. And poor Sam was being unwillingly seduced by Charlie's old girlfriend Naomi. Everyone was shocked, and the pastor's wife fainted. Much to her credit, Mrs. Felcher later downplayed the incident, understanding that Machiko had yet to learn many American customs. (MACHIKO)

Feminine Mystique, The

Betty Freidan's book is widely credited with starting the Women's Liberation movement. Emma Rickett was reading and learning from this tome on her family vacation. (RUNAWAY)

Fergeson, Chip, Ensign (US Navy)

He and Al were tail-pipe buddies. Chip took Marci Riker out to the beach in Bingo's car, and it was he the commander saw instead of Bingo. Years later Chip caught a SAM missile over Hai Phong and died during the Vietnam War. (LISA)

Fermi Suit

A special suit that has to be worn in order to leap. It looks like a white turtleneck body-suit. The name comes from Enrico Fermi, who established the theory of beta decay and discovered the statistical laws that are obeyed by elementary particles. Fermi also built the first nuclear reactor, then moved to Los Alamos (not far from the site of Project Quantum Leap) to help develop the atomic bomb. (BACK)

Fireman

Sam was one when he rescued a cat named Ginger in 1957 during a leap shown on the first run of *Honeymoon Express* (HONEYMOON

Fletcher, Paula

She and her fiancé Kevin Wentworth had had a big fight before Kevin went out with Katie McBain in an attempt to make her jealous. (RAPED)

Foghorn Motel

Murderer Tony Besh hid out at this San Francisco motel. (EYES)

Ford, Gerald

Sam's being able to predict when the president was going to take a little "trip" helped convince Chris Stone's father that he could see the future, and thus Chad could become a singer instead of a stunt man like his dad. (DISCO)

Fort Cronkite

Katie McBain was raped at this isolated spot. (RAPED)

Foster, Vanessa

The Philadelphia Fosters had more dough than Pillsbury, and as a result, Vanessa had grown up the quintessential spoiled brat. Her father owned the largest shipping line in the US, but wasn't going to be there for her wedding because he had a stockholders' meeting. Her fiancée David was just like her father, wanting to give her material possessions instead of love. Vanessa was on a yacht and about to get married when she snuck a cigarette near the engine room, tossing the butt in a bucket of oil rags. The ship exploded. Despite her upbringing, she found herself attracted to Nikos Stathatos, a Greek sailor who worked in the engine room and rescued her after the explosion. Originally she still married David, but Sam leaped into Nikos and, being no sailor, got them marooned on a desert island where they stayed for nine years and had six kids. (SHREW)

Fourcade, Marsha

For lack of a better word, the "madam" of the LaBonte "house". She was engaged to Gilbert LaBonte, and when Sam leaped in she gave him a "preview" of LaBonte's birthday present. Marsha was the type of girl some would consider "fast" when she was growing up, and left Lake Charles, Louisiana to become a "working girl". Still, she regretted her life and wanted to start over, and saw marriage to LaBonte as part of that start. Her fear though is that Gilbert would see her as nothing but a whore. She ended up going to Atlanta, to live with her cousin Gina, who was four months pregnant and had escaped from an abusive husband. (COMFORT)

Fox, Tim "Foxy"

Thirty-two-year-old third baseman for the Waco Bombers. Fox hit .415 in 1963 and got called up to Chicago where he broke his leg sliding into 2nd, and got sent back down to recover. That was five years before Sam leaped into him during the ninth inning of the final game of the season. Tim was supposed to retire and open up a Kentucky Fried Chicken franchise. The Bombers were going to end the year in the cellar again if they didn't win. Sam ends up with an inside-the-park homer of sorts. Sam found himself facing future pitching legend Tom Seaver, whose fast ball Sam hadn't a prayer of hitting. The catcher missed the ball on the last strike, though, and Sam rounded the bases as the Killeen team made tons of errors. He slid into home safely and won the game. (PILOT)

Frank

Bartender at The Roadside Rendezvous near Tullarosa, NM. He died in a car bomb meant for Joey DeNardo. (PIANO)

Freddy

A young orderly at Havenwell Hospital who was also a medical student. He remarked that people get committed and then go crazy. (SHOCK)

Frost, Diane

Wanted in Arkansas for embezzlement, she was being escorted home by bounty hunter Gordon O'Reilly. She protested her innocence to Gordon/Sam, explaining that when she found out her boss was running a phony gold share scheme she forged her name to one million dollars in checks, intending to refund the money to the investors, including her mother. Diane was one big bundle of trouble for Sam, trying every scheme she could think of in order to gain her freedom, which didn't help Sam believe her story. Finally the truth came to the surface, and Sam helped her recover the checks. The charges against her were dropped, and Diane Frost became one of the best bounty hunters in the business. (HUNT)

Fuller, Abagail

The whole town believed this little girl was cursed crazy because her mother and her grandmother were "touched". When Sam leaped into her father Clayton, Abagail had just found the body of Bart Aider, father of Violet, a girl Abagail had been accused of murdering two years before. The girls had gotten into a fight over a locket, and Abagail said Violet had run off and that was the last she had seen of her. Violet's body was never found, but her bloody sweater was. Clayton was the sheriff, and he closed the case, saying a pack of wild dogs must have killed the girl. Violet's mother Leta never stopped haranguing Abagail, insisting she killed Violet. And when her husband Bart died under mysterious circumstances, she believed Abagail killed him, too. Leta tried to get Abagail to admit she killed Violet, and then set the Fuller house on fire, hoping to kill Abagail. Sam rescued Abagail and leaped just before Clayton was killed.

Cut to 1966. Twenty-one-year-old Abagail was preparing to marry Will Kinman, the local deputy. Sam leaped into Will the night before the wedding, and she later told him that making love seemed wrong and then in a "magic flash" it was though their bodies were made for each other.

Sam was equally attracted to Abagail, practically becoming obsessed with her. When a boy she had been baby-sitting disappeared, the town – at Leta's instigation – blamed her and formed a lynch mob. Sam kept Abagail from being shot, and helped the town find the missing boy.

Cut to 1978. Violet Aider's bones were found at the bottom of the town well during restoration work. Leta went to an attorney, who told her they couldn't prosecute because Abagail was a minor when the crime occurred. Later, Leta's body was found on Abagail's kitchen floor. Abagail was arrested an, in the original history, died in the electric chair on June 30, 1984. Sam leaped into Larry Stanton, a former local attorney who had moved to Shreveport. The Fuller family housekeeper asked Sam to take the case, and he did. Sam was surprised to meet Sammie Jo, Abagail's daughter by Will Kinman. She and Will never married, and she raised the child on her own. Al reported that Sammie Joe was conceived while Sam was Will Kinman. Sm proved Abagail's innocence by showing that Leta Aider had called the police before committing suicide in the kitchen. Abagail eventually married, moved to Chicago, and is happy to this day. (TRILOGY)

Fuller, Clayton

Sam found himself as this LA sheriff with a murder investigation on his hands. He and his daughter Abagail were going to die in a house fire on August 9, 1955 unless he changed history. The fire was started by Leta Aider, who lured Abagail to the house. Sam rescued Abagail and leaped seconds before Clayton died. (TRILOGY)

Fuller, Laura (née Blanchette)

Clayton Fuller's wife. When Sam leaped in, he thought Laura was dead, but saw a "vision" of her when a gust of wind blew open his bedroom door. He found out from Abagail that the night Violet Aider died they had a terrible argument and she left. Sam found she had been committed to Peach Hill Home for the Mentally Ill that night. He visited and found her uncommunicative, rocking and staring into space, though she did seem to notice Al.

When Sam visited her eleven years later as Will Kinman, Laura wore bandages on her head and one arm. She was more communicative, but talked about her mother, who had killed all of her brothers and sisters because there was no food. She had escaped death because she had fallen under the bed. She saw Sam as himself and believed he would keep her daughter safe.

In 1978 when Abagail was being held for Leta Aider's murder, Sam went back to visit Laura as Larry Stanton. The bandages were gone, revealing a head and arm that had been severely burned. Her doctor said she was staying at the hospital of her own accord and was free to come and go as she pleased. Laura remembered him as Sam, and said that Clayton told her he would come, and now she would tell the whole truth about Violet Aider's death. She had seen Violet after the fight, and the girl backed away and fell into a well. Laura tried to catch her, but was only able to grab the locket. Since Laura wasn't at the hospital against her will, here testimony on Abagail's behalf was accepted in court. (TRILOGY)

Fuller, Lester "Doc"

Thirty-five-year-old pitcher for the Galveston Mustangs minor league baseball team. Fuller had once been the dominant pitcher in the game as a player for the Cubs, but he hit a batter in the head with a pitch and the batter died. They didn't wear batting helmets in those days. Ziggy gives Sam an 89% probability that he's there to help Doc get back into the major leagues, but Sam suspected he was there for Chuckie Myerwich, a hot pitcher and an angry young man. A Yankees scout offered Chuckie a chance at the majors and Doc a position as a pitching coach. (BALL)

Fuller, Samantha Josephine (Sammie Jo)

She looked just like her mother Abagail did when she was a girl, but Ziggy gave a 91.9% chance that she was Sam's daughter and not Will Kinman's. Like her daddy, she has a photographic memory, and while her IQ of 194 is not as high as Sam's, it is still pretty impressive. *Brigadoon* is her favorite book, and was also Sam's. She told Sam she wanted to go back in time so she could meet her daddy and tell him that she loved him. In the original history she was so traumatized by the death of her mother that she dropped out and ended up living in Mobile writing manuals for a small computer company. At Abagail's trial she screamed out that she had seen everything, and told how Leta killed herself. Now her own history has changed and she's working for Project Quantum Leap, and even has a theory on how to bring Sam home. She doesn't know Sam is her father. (TRILOGY)

G

Gable, Clark

Marilyn Monroe's co-star in *The Misfits*. (NORMA)

Galatians 5:7-10

When, as a lawyer in 1957, Sam had trouble getting some people to testify on behalf of his client, he found that they had sworn on a Bible to tell a different version of the story, and believed that if they swore on a Bible on the stand to tell the real story they would go to Hell. Sam used these verses to show them the light: "You were running well; who hindered you from obeying the truth? This persuasion is not from him who called you. A little leaven leavens the whole lump. I have confidence in the Lord that you will take no view other than mine; and he who is troubling you will bear his judgment, whoever he is." (HELP)

Genetic Field Transference

Sam's theory as to why he leaped into John Beckett during the Civil War. He postulated (and Ziggy confirmed) that somehow he could leap along his own DNA and into his ancestors. (STATES)

George

Marilyn Monroe's agent (NORMA). Michael Blake's driver was also named George (MIRACLE).

Georgia Wrestle-a-thon.

A big wrestling meet in Atlanta in 1955. Sam leaped into the middle of one of the matches. (CHAMP)

Ghost of Christmas Future

Since Michael Blake's neurons and mesons were close in frequency to Sam's, Al was able to present himself to the millionaire as the Ghost of Christmas Future. Dressed in pale makeup, chains and an ugly shabby suit, he appeared before Blake and showed him his future. (MIRACLE)

Giovanni, Jimmy

Troian Claridge's brother had made himself her caretaker after her husband Julian died, gaining power of attorney and sending her to many doctors to attempt to get her over her depression stemming from her loss. He turned out to be quite an electronics genius, rigging up a gang-loaded series of tape players with "Julian's voice" played at a very high frequency. High enough for her to hear, but not for most other people. He was trying to drive her to suicide so he could gain complete control of her money. (TROIAN)

Glasserman, Bert

He claimed that he was writing a book, that he had been a widower for two years and that his wife's name was Delores. His book was about the loss of a loved one, he said, and he really wanted to talk to Irene Besh about the loss of her son Danny.

In truth Glasserman had never married, and Al found a copy of his book, *Women in Paris*. Irene is chapter 6. It was a best-seller in the 1970s. His "widowhood" was just a come-on to women. After Irene learned the truth she told one of her friends, and he got hit with a libel suit and the publisher suspended publication of the book. (SHALT)

'Glory of Love, The'

Sam dedicated this song he played over WOF to the girl he most wanted to share a Civil defense shelter with, then proceeded to dance with Rachel Porter and charm her socks off. (PEORIA)

Goat

Sam saw a goat when Tully McKnight died. He said it yanked on a rag tied to the ladder. The nearest farm was 15 miles from where Joshua Rey lived, though. Later, he swerved to avoid a goat on the road, and then saw one at the scene of Ben Masters' Death. (BMAN)

God, Time and Whoever

Sam and Al theorized that God was somehow controlling the leaps. That was the only possible explanation they could find. Ziggy also proposed this theory after Sam first leaped. (MIRACLE)

After leaping into a bar called Al's Place in Cokeburg, PA, Sam began to believe that the enigmatic bartender was God, or Time or whoever was leaping him around in time. Al the bartender, on the other hand, tried to convince Sam that he was responsible for his own destiny. (MIRROR)

Gomez

Kid Cody's trainer was a "rum dumb" ex-fighter who used to take dives. He was tired of training crooked fighters, and didn't believe Kid Cody/Sam at first when he told him that he wanted to go legit. Ultimately he did train Sam for the championship fight. (HAND)

Good Morning, Vietnam

When Sam found it impossible to be a DJ, Al asked if he remembered this movie. Sam proceeded to do an incredible Robin Williams impression. (PEORIA)

Gooshie

Head programmer at Project Quantum Leap. He also works the controls for the Imaging Chamber. He made a frantic call to Al when Sam leaped the first time. Gooshie is described as a short guy with bad breath (PILOT). He and Tina once had an affair, and when Sam briefly changed history, they were married (TESS, LISA). While playing poker, Sam covered up an exclamation about Gooshie by saying "Gooshie" was Navajo for "I'll see it" (TESS). Al once called him "jockstrap-breath".

Gooshie a bit absent-minded. When Leon Styles escorted Al into the hallway at gun point, Gooshie just looked up and acknowledged "Dr. Beckett". He drives a blue Ford Probe, which he got after his car had been stolen the year before. At Al's suggestion, he had a tracking device installed in his new car and was able to redirect its signal so Ziggy could track it after Styles took the vehicle. (KILLIN)

Gooshie was also the name of the old mailman in the town of Cokeburg, PA. Coincidentally, he also had bad breath. (MIRROR)

Grady

Best friend of "Black Magic" Walters, he is perhaps the only man other than Walters himself (and Al when he was a kid) who is allowed to touch Alberta. He's a bit naive, letting one of Eddie Davis's boys lure him out into the alley in order to break the legendary stick. He gives Sam his own stick, Bathsheba, so he can finish the match. (POOL)

Granson, Karl

Sam leaped into this high-fashion photographer in 1965. After some coaxing from Al, he took pretty well to the role, likening it to "painting with people". Karl is from Queens, and apparently was known to pop a few pills himself, which made it more difficult for Sam to moralize about drugs. (STROBE)

'Great Balls of Fire'

Sam wowed the crowd at the Miss Deep South pageant with this song to clinch the beauty contest title. (SOUTH)

Greely, Mary

Organist and deacon at Coventry Presbyterian Church and part-time research assistant to writer Joshua Rey, to whom she was engaged. Al/Boogieman told Sam that she was originally found strangled in the church spook house on Halloween, 1964. Al/Boogieman kept telling Sam that she was responsible for a bizarre series of murders that were taking place on that day. As proof of her supposed powers, a skull flew across the room while she suffered an epileptic seizure. Sam pointed out that, while very rare, telekenetic incidents had been linked to seizures. Her address was 966 Salem Avenue, and when Al passed through the door, the 9 turned upside-down. (BMAN)

Green, Marsha

Sat right in front of Sam in the fourth grade. (DOUBLE)

Greenman, Lenny

He was hoping his son Max could achieve the dream that had eluded him for 42 years – that of having his own cab. He had worked for Frank O'Connor's father, but when the son took over the business he put the elder Greenman out to pasture. When Lenny found out that Frank cheated him out of his medallion, he left his insurance policy out, took his gun, and confronted Frank. Sam saved Lenny, and although he was charged with a crime, he received probation and he and Max had their cab company. (WONDERFUL)

Greenman, Max

Sam leaped into this New York cabby on May 10, 1958. Max was just $50 short of winning a contest sponsored by his employer, which would get him his own medallion so he could go into business for himself. (WONDERFUL)

Greer, Mandy

Her sister was one of the hostages in the bank robbery in Elk Ridge. Mandy was a classmate of the man Sam had leaped into, William Walters, but Sam also remembered her. In high school she wore braces and a patch over her eye, and played Captain Hook in the school production of Peter Pan. The braces eventually came off. (LAND)

Gretze, Hannah

She was in Al's fourth grade class. He explained that he used to dip her pigtails into the inkwell until he discovered it was a lot more fun to take her into the cloakroom. When Sam started at that revelation, Al shrugged and explained that he was "socially advanced". (DOUBLE)

Griggs, John, Dr.

Sam called in the ring physician for the Georgia Wrestle-a-thon to give Ronnie Sammis a complete physical. His aim was to prove Ronnie had a heart condition and shouldn't wrestle. All the doctor did was take the wrestler's blood pressure and listen to his chest. While he found a little congestion in the lungs, there was nothing he could see that would keep Ronnie from going into the ring. (CHAMP)

Grimsley, Allison

Widow of Nick Allen's partner Phil. Allison was 16 when she met Phil when he was in Pittsburgh for a divorce case. She was the daughter of a steel worker, and his apparent sophistication swept her off her feet. She never loved him and in fact fell for Nick Allen. They were seeing each other, but never slept together as they both felt it was wrong. Allison was a redhead and quite alluring. Al described her as having a body that could part the Red Army. (SEYMOUR)

Grimwald, Deke, Col. (USAF)

He brought Maggie Dawson to Tom's S.E.A.L. unit with instructions that she was to accompany them on a mission the next day. His dad was General Max Grimwald. (NAM)

Grumman Goose

The plane Sam was co-piloting through the Bermuda Triangle. They had been used in World War II to help track down German U-boats. This one had been converted for executive use. (SHIP)

Gulf View Apartments

Sam had to evacuate a hurricane party from a condo there, as Archie Necaise had in the original history, saving twelve lives. (HURRICANE)

Gulfport Bank

Since it was two blocks away from the Gulf View Apartments and several people had survived hurricane Camille inside in the original history, Sam evacuated the hurricane party at the apartments to this building. (HURRICANE)

Gunfighter, The

A hotel in the Texas panhandle where Sam and Bunny O'Hare stopped briefly to feed and change Christie Dalton. (MAYBE)

Gutierrez, Roberto Roberto

Host of the talk show *Roberto!* on KDNM Channel 2 in Destiny, NM in 1982. Gutierrez specialized in sleazy topics, but after Sam leaped in he took up fellow reporter Jani Eisenberg's bet that he couldn't do a decent story. As a result Roberto/Sam exposed a fertilizer company making illegal chemical weapons. Sam ended Roberto's show with a tease stating soon he would tell the audience about "the time I was kidnapped by aliens and held in an all-white room". (ROBERTO)

Haller, Eugene B.

The judge in Twelve Oaks, Louisiana who was presiding over the trial of Lila Barry. (HELP)

Hammond, Mike

As president of the Chi Kappa Delta fraternity, he instituted a deadly hazing ritual for new members. Arnold Watkins/Sam's actions got the fraternity suspended. After Hammond tried to kill Arnold/Sam, he was expelled from college, and even his dad wouldn't hire him. (RETURN)

Hardin, Dr.

Investigator with Project Blue Book checking out Max Stoddard. He used sodium pentathol to see if Stoddard was indeed telling the truth, and since Sam had leaped into Stoddard he heard Sam's tale of time travel. (BRIGHT)

Harker Falls

Thirty miles from Elk Ridge, Indiana. Gus Vernon had to be brought back from there after his bank had been robbed. (LAND)

Harper, Lonnie

Since he was putting his brother Ray through medical school, Lonnie was doubly upset that Ray was dating a white girl and didn't want to stay in Watts to help his own people. After the riots ensued and Poppa Dee was killed, he took Susan Brewster hostage and threatened to kill her unless black people stopped dying. A futile act, but Sam convinced Lonnie to release Susan. Seconds later, a police sniper killed Lonnie. (B&W)

Harper, Momma

Ray and Lonnie's mother was on a bus when the Watts Riots started, and the bus was attacked. The family is from Mariposa, and she observes that no matter what they do, they can't get away from the hate. (B&W)

Harper, Ray

Sam leaped into this Watts medical student on August 11, 1965, the day the deadly riots began. Harper was a brilliant student and had been offered an internship in Boston. He was considering taking it because it would be easier to continue his relationship with Susan Brewster, who happened to be white. Originally, he lost her because of the riots, and then lost his dream of becoming a doctor. After Sam's intervention in the riots, Ray and Susan became doctors and opened a clinic in Watts. (B&W)

Harriet

One of the milk cows at the Beckett farm. Most likely named after Harriet Margulies, executive assistant to Donald P. Bellisario. (HOME)

Harris, Ben

Writer for the *Time Patrol* program, and also all–round producer/director at a TV station in St. Louis. He used to work in radio. The stuff he writes seems pretty much like schlock, but it was standard 1950s fare. (FUTURE)

Hart, Kyle

Known as "Dr. Hunk" to his fans, Hart played Dr. Craig Conner on the soap opera *Moments to Live.* Sam leaped into Hart just in time to have lunch with Norma Jean Pilcher, winner of a soap contest, who then kidnapped Kyle/Sam and wanted to force him to father her child. After Sam convinced Norma Jean she was doing the wrong thing, Hart's agent decided it would be a good idea to use the events in Craig Conner's storyline. (MOMENTS)

Hartig, James, Commander

Officer in charge of the veterans' hospital in San Diego. (NOWHERE)

Hartman, Phil

Owned Phil's, the pharmacy next door to the ritzy Bianca salon in Beverly Hills. He seemed to be a pretty good guy:

President of the Rotary Club, sang in the Baptist choir. Phil had declared bankruptcy in early 1982, but later paid his creditors off with interest. When he died he had $200,000 in the bank. It turned out Hartman was selling drugs to Chloe, who was selling them to Bianca's customers. After Hartman got himself out of debt he decided he had had enough and wanted out, and got murdered. (PERM)

Havenwell Hospital

Pennsylvania mental hospital where Sam received a high dose of shock therapy, which caused him to assume the personalities of people into which he had leaped. (SHOCK)

Heimlich, Dr.

Sam saved him from choking on February 3, 1974. (SHALT)

Henderson's Bakery

Michael Blake had put a lot of people, including at least one childhood friend, out of work when he purchased this bakery. In 1962 United Federal wanted to buy the company because Blake "had the guts and fortitude" to automate it. (MIRACLE)

Hendrix, Jimi

Sam tried to tell Tim Stoddard about this rock guitarist, but it was still a year before he would burst on the scene. Instead, Sam grabbed Tim's electric guitar and did a passable impression of the guitarist's feedback-laden style, playing 'The Battle Hymn of the Republic'. (BRIGHT)

Heywood, Stephanie

She and Hilla Danner were very close friends. Stephanie wanted to be a photographer, and took many photos of Hilla. They had made plans to go to New York together, with Hilla as her model. She was jealous of Greg Truesdale's relationship with Hilla, and thought Hilla didn't love her any more. They had an argument, and she drove the spiked heel of her shoe into Hilla's skull, killing her. (DEAR)

Hieroglyphics

Sam can read them, having a degree in Archaeology and a life-long insterest in Egyptology. Al once used hieroglyphics printed on a robe to convey to Sam information about Donna's father he couldn't otherwise say because the Committee was looking on. In a later leap he easily deciphered the symbols depicting the curse of King Ptah-Hotep II. (CROSSED, CURSE)

Hill, Alexandra

Nigel Corrington had recently married this young homeless girl, and when Sam leaped into Corrington it was to stop her death. She knew she was taking part in the Blood Moon ritual, but seemed to have no idea she was to be the sacrifice, as the next day her body was found in the forest, completely drained of blood. Fearing what Nigel might do upon his return, Sam sent her away once he had thwarted the ritual. Alexandra ended up becoming a street missionary. (BLOOD)

Hill, Anita

She watched and listened intently as Sam, in the persona of Dr. Ruth Westheimer, talked to Jonathan Holmby about sexual harassment. (RUTH)

Hill, Cheri

Ray Harper's ex-girlfriend, who called him "Dr. Strange-love" and used to help him with his anatomy lessons. (B&W)

Hill, Clint

Jackie Kennedy's Secret Service agent. Sam leaped into him on the grassy knoll, presumably to save Jackie's life. (LHO)

Hillview

Prescott Naval Academy was preparing for a track meet against this school when Sam leaped into Tommy York in 1964. (HONOR)

Holding Chamber

The name for the Waiting Room at the time travel project controlled by Lothos. (REVENGE)

Holly, Buddy

When Sam leaped into a Texas panhandle veterinarian in 1956, Holly was his assistant. Sam didn't leap until he had helped Holly with the lyrics to 'Peggy Sue'. (TESS)

Holmby, Jonathan

Annie Wilkins' boss at the law firm where she worked as a secretary had been sexually harassing her since day one. After Sam helped her quit her job, Holmby accused Annie of making the advances. Later, Holmby confronted Annie at her apartment with the intention of teaching her a lesson. He would have killed her had Sam not intervened. (RUTH)

Hologram, Neuro

Sam and Al both see each other as holograms. Sam describes the link thusly: "Created by subatomic agitation of carbon quarks tuned to the mesons of my optic and otic neurons." During his first leap, Sam called Al a vampire because he did not reflect in a mirror. (PILOT)

Almost all animals can see Al (TESS). Once he managed to "get through" to at least one elderly person. Melanie Trafford didn't see him, but apparently did hear him, although she believed she was hearing her dead husband (COLOR). Joseph Washakie also heard Al the day before he died (FREEDOM). As Maggie Dawson died, she also saw Al, and apparently recognized him as one of the POWs she had just photographed (NAM). A fortune teller at a circus who apparently had some psychic powers could sense Al's presence, though not see or hear him (NET).

Al's voice was amplified through some "ghostbusting" equipment designed by Dr. Timothy Mintz. It was designed to pick up a wide spectrum of electrical activity. He used the equipment to tell Troian Claridge not to kill herself. Her brother Jimmy heard Al's voice too, but believed it was a gimmick cooked up by Dr. Mintz. (TROIAN)

Because kids under the age of five exist in a natural alpha

state, they can see Al. Both kids and animals are pure of heart, and see only the truth, which is that Al is present with Sam. He used a young girl at a church to guide Tearsa Lorrea to the spot where a bullet had been lodged in a wall. The girl believed Al was an angel. (LAST, MOTHER, JUSTICE)

Psychic Tamlyn Matsuda could feel something whenever Al was present. Once it was a strange energy, another time it was a chill (EYES). Angela, the woman who claimed to be an angel, could also see him (WONDERFUL). Sam could hear Al's voice over the telephone. Al was with Tearsa Lorrea and told Sam to warn her that someone was coming (LAST). Laura Fuller could see Al (TRILOGY).

The "mentally absent" can see Al, which meant Tibby and half the residents at Havenwell. When Sam's mental condition deteriorated, Al had more trouble maintaining contact. (SHOCK)

Another group of people who can see and hear Al are those whose neurons and mesons are on a frequency close to Sam's. Michael Blake saw Al, and Ziggy was able to shift Al's image to a frequency Sam could pick up but not Blake. Al likened it to tuning a radio. (MIRACLE)

When Sam was working on the transmitter at WOF, Al got too close and began to glow blue. Al thought he was leaping, but Sam explained it was just the effect from the transmitter (PEORIA). Al's holographic image also glowed when he stood under a black light in a restaurant (CROSSED).

Gooshie was able to contact Al in the "present" as a sort of hologram. Al could hear the programmer but not see him. Gooshie reported that was because Ziggy had trouble getting their brainwaves synched. Al took that as a compliment. (KILLIN)

While the Project was designed around Sam and Al's brainwaves, Ziggy can put another person in contact with

Sam, although the results may not be as good. When Gooshie had to step in for Al once, the connection was rather tenuous. (KILLIN)

Hopper, Dennis

While cheering the Elk Ridge Cougars on from the side of the basketball court (albeit holographically), Al said he felt like Hopper in *Hoosiers*. (HOME)

Horst

Nigel Corrington's butler fit the stereotype of the creepy Transylvanian manservant. It was he who saved Sam's life after being dismissed for the evening and returning to retrieve his hat. (BLOOD)

How to Spot a Vampire

Al quoted from chapter six of Dr. Laszlo Fang's book: "Vampires are not merely bloodsuckers. They are sexually obsessed and many of them possess insatiable carnal urges beyond the grave." Sam pointed out that vampires and holograms have a lot in common. (BLOOD)

Howell, "Howlin'" Chick

Having worked a dozen jobs in the previous twelve years, Howell ended up at WOF in Peoria. After Howell/Sam helped the station in its crusade to play rock and roll, he stayed. A year later he and station-owner Rachel Porter married. (PEORIA)

Hoyt, John

Since Leon Styles murdered his daughter, the local sheriff was out to "return the favor". In the original history, he did kill Styles, but Carol Pruitt convinced him that he would ruin his own life if he didn't let justice take its course. (KILLIN)

Hudson, Nancy

The assistant District Attorney handling Katie McBain's rape case. At first she tried to convince Katie that it would be rough to prosecute because the teenager and the rapist were friends. After she lost the case, she confessed that she had been raped twelve years earlier and since then only tried to take cases that she thought she could win because she went through it all again whenever she lost. They never caught the man that raped her. (RAPED)

Huston, John

The noted film director was at the helm of the film that eventually became *The Misfits*. (NORMA)

Hutton, Ray

Sam leaped into the understudy for Don Quixote in *The Man of La Mancha* moments before he was to go onstage in Syracuse. Fortunately for Sam, the star, John O'Malley, showed up seconds before he was to make his entrance. Although he was inebriated, O'Malley performed brilliantly. The closest Hutton ever got to stardom was as understudy for O'Malley. (CATCH)

Hydell, Alex James (Alik)

One of the actual aliases Lee Harvey Oswald used, and the name he gave to Al in the Waiting Room. Oswald used that alias to buy a gun he took to the Texas Schoolbook Depository. Oswald/Sam also used the alias in New Orleans. In the Waiting Room, Oswald gave that name to Al as the one who would shoot JFK. (LHO)

Imaging Chamber

Sam and Al share a mental link through Ziggy, who has tuned their neurons and mesons together. An implant may also be involved in the process. Once inside, Al can see things within a certain unspecified range of Sam although the surroundings are like a hologram – he cannot touch anything. (PILOT)

The Imaging Chamber is lined with radium rings. If a catastrophic collapse were suffered, the door would be automatically sealed and would not be reopened for 1600 years, the half-life of the ring. (BACK)

Should someone get trapped, there is enough air to sustain life for one person for six months, although food may be another question. The door can be activated one of two ways: either through the handlink or the console outside of the room. (BACK)

When not in use, the Imaging Chamber is the same blue as the Waiting Room. When Al activates the link, an image forms from a disc above his head and radiates downward. As they try to get a fix on Sam, images swirl around Al until they lock in on the specific time and place. (MIRROR)

When Al and Sam simo-leaped, the handlink went with Al, trapping Sam. Sam suggested Al sent a note to the Beckett family attorney to be delivered on September 18, 1999 to the Project. Gooshie thought the idea was brilliant, and told Sam it took 54 years, 7 months and six days for the note to reach its ultimate destination. (BACK)

Whenever Al touches something or someone while inside the Imaging Chamber, the object or person becomes visible to Sam (BLIND, SHOCK). At first if another person was in the Imaging Chamber touching Al, Sam could see but not hear. After Sam leaped into rape victim Katie McBain, it was very important that he hear her story in her own words so he could testify at the trial, so Al and Ziggy rigged up a way to make it possible, but it took enough power to light St. Louis for a month. (RAPED)

While the observer can hear Ziggy speaking to him, the leaper cannot hear the computer's voice. (BACK)

Italian

One language Sam cannot speak. Al had to tell him what to say to Don Geno Prascotti. (DOUBLE)

J

Jackson, Bob

An employee for the Rosenfeld and Adams ad agency, he saw Joe Thurlow/Sam playing Hamlet in the nude and offered him the job of the Boxer Boy in the underwear ads. (PLAY)

Jackson, Michael

Sam ran into a very young Michael in 1961 when he and his brothers were doing a show at the same hotel where Cheryl Wilson's rehearsal dinner was being held. Sam taught him how to moonwalk. (CAM)

Jackson, Tiger Joe

Kid Cody/Sam had to fight him for the Heavyweight Championship of California. Shady promoter Jake Edwards had paid Cody to take a dive in the first round, but Sam was determined to win. He eventually did. (HAND)

Jacobs, Brenda

She did the news for a station in Buffalo, and in the original history married Doug Bridges because she thought it would do her career some good. They got divorced in six months and she married a game show host. When she finally got her first big assignment, she blew it and ended up writing for a retirement newspaper. We were never told what happened after history was altered and Doug stayed with Debbie Schafer. (RUTH)

Jarret, Tom, Captain (US Army)

When Sam and Al simo-leaped, Al landed in this World War II vet who had just arrived home in Crown Point, Indiana on June 15, 1945. Jarret had spent the last three years in a POW camp, and his apparent death had been mentioned in one of Ernie Pyle's newspaper columns. His birthday is in April, and he's a recipient of the Congressional Medal of Honor. In the original history, he and his fiancée Suzanne apparently committed suicide, but it was actually engineered by Clifford, the man Suzanne had pledged to marry after Jarret was given up for dead. (BACK)

Jenkins, Victoria

Miss Confederacy in the Miss Deep South beauty pageant. Her goals included helping the needy and singing in the church choir. She was the first runner-up (to her disappointment) and won a $1,000 scholarship. (SOUTH)

Jenelle

She hung out at The Roadside Rendezvous near Tullarosa, NM where Chuck Tanner played piano under the name of Joey DeNardo. She died in a car bombing meant for Joey. (PIANO)

Jenson, Angela (Angel)

Never get busted for selling pot in an election year. That was the lesson intended when this nineteen-year-old was sent to Mallard Prison. When Alia and Sam leaped together, she found herself as Angel. Sam hypnotized her into believing she actually was the inmate in the hope that Lothos would be unable to get a lock on her brainwaves. (REVENGE)

Jill

Sixteen-year-old tomboy who had a crush on Cameron Wilson. She was just as thrilled to work on cars as Cam was, and he was also attracted to her. Sam leaped out as she and Cam/Sam shared a first kiss. (CAM)

Jimenez, Angelita Carmen Guadalupe Cecilia

When Sam leaped into a New York cab driver in 1958, he ran right over Angela in the middle of 34th street. Angela didn't suffer a scratch, and told Sam she was his guardian angel. Angela was dressed as a flapper, and it was later discovered that a woman of her name was known in the 1920s Spanish Harlem as "the Puerto Rican Fanny Brice". She died while singing at an audition after she hit the high note and fell fifteen feet into the pits. Angela explained that they told her in Heaven that she was too vain in life and had a big ego, so she had to learn humility by helping others. Every time she helps someone, she says, she moves on to her next assignment. No one remembers she was there, she claims.

Angel or not, Angela could see Al. Al chalked that up to her being loco.

After Angela took a bullet during a robbery, she stood up and showed no sign of a wound. Sam found entry and exit holes in her coat, but no evidence of injury. After Sam accomplished his mission, Angela told him it was time for her to go, and called him by his true name rather than the name of the man he had leaped into. Sam forgot her, but Al didn't because he was in the future. (WONDERFUL)

Jimmerson, Fedelia (Fiddler)

A hearing-impaired inmate at Mallard Prison who was in on charges of kidnapping. It turned out to be a case of mistaken identity, and she was released six years later and disappeared. She had some crucial evidence to clear Liz Tate of Carol Bening's murder. (REVENGE)

Joda

A large Japanese transvestite who ran a bar where a lot of Marines, including Lee Harvey Oswald, hung out. (LHO)

John

The mailboy at National Motors preferred the ladies to call him "Big John". Sam just wanted to break his face. (GLORIA)

Johnson, Betsy

Ultra-rich Vanessa Foster's one middle-class friend. (SHREW)

Johnson, Tibido (Tibby)

A mild form of Down's syndrome coupled with a series of bad headaches got this young man a trip to Havenwell when he was a child. Sam's job was to teach him to read so he could be a productive member of society when he was released in 1962. While Tibby was mildly retarded, he could remember some things like music very well, learning the words to 'Pigsfoot Pete' and 'Scrub Me Momma With the Boogie Beat' the very first time he heard them. Since Sam was in no condition to teach Tibby how to read, Al made up a rap song to teach Tibby the alphabet. This was the foundation he needed to learn to read. Because Tibby was still very child-like, he could see Al. (SHOCK)

Johnson, Sgt. William (Billy)

After a Vietcong sniper's bullet severed his spinal cord and left him paralyzed from the neck down, Billy felt no reason to live and was sabotaging his life. When his fiancée Carol came to visit, he turned her away, believing perhaps that it was easier to die if no one was there to care for him. In the original history, he killed himself by drowning in the hospital swimming pool. Sam let him go under, telling Al the only way the man could live was if he wanted to, then rescued Johnson after he'd had a few long seconds to think about what he had done. (NOWHERE)

K

KCB Radio

Located Victorville at 530 on the AM dial. Tom/Sam and Peg Stratton listened to this station in the car. The group playing was Velton Bunch and the Dovetones. (PILOT)

KDNM-TV

Channel 2 in Destiny, NM, home of *Roberto!* (ROBERTO)

KHOI

When Sam first leaped into Tom Stratton, his son was watching *Howdy Doody* on KHOI-TV. (PILOT)

KRVA-TV

Sam first saw what Leon Styles looked like when his face was shown on a newscast on this station. (KILLIN)

KSFW-TV, Channel 12

Reporter Dylan Powell worked at this San Francisco station. (EYES)

Kathy

Chimp #90 ended up in Cory's cage after Cory was taken to Dr. Winger. (WRONG)

Keeter

Dotty Billings' boyfriend didn't seem to amount to much, but he was all she had, and she was afraid to risk losing him by keeping Billie Jean and her baby. When the girl went into labor, Keeter refused to take her to the hospital. (8½)

Keisker, Marion

Worked at Sun Records' scouting talent. Sam had to impress her at a talent show in order to secure an audition for Elvis Presley. (MEMPHIS)

Kennedy, Jackie

Sam leaped into Secret Service agent Clint Hill in time to prevent the First Lady from being killed along with her husband. (LHO)

Kennedy, John F.

Sam leaped out of Lee Harvey Oswald just before Oswald pulled the trigger to assassinate the president (LHO). He's most likely the senator from Massachusetts alluded to when Sam was Marilyn Monroe's driver. Peter Lawford mentioned this senator was his brother-in-law, so in all likelihood it was Kennedy (NORMA). Mac Ellroy's family was watching his televised talk on the Cuban Missile Crisis on October 27, 1962 when a blackout took place and the sirens began to wail (NUCLEAR).

Kenu

Shoshone for grandfather. (FREEDOM)

Kerouac, Jack

Legendary Beat writer and author of *On the Road*, a sort of Bible to the motorcycle types. He lived in a cabin near Big Sur. (REBEL)

Kiner, Irene

Moe Stein's daughter was trying to have him committed because she believed him to be a danger to himself. She lived in Milwaukee, and just felt she couldn't be there for him all of the time. In the end she let her dad come live with her. (FUTURE)

King, Isaac

After every slave ran away from the Covington plantation, why was this one still hanging on? Isaac was manning a stop on the Underground Railway while Olivia Covington looked the other way. He found John Beckett/Sam passed out and bleeding and brought him back to the plantation. After he fled the place with Olivia and John/Sam, he decided his free name would be Isaac King, because he felt like one. One of his descendants was Martin Luther King. (STATES)

King, Stephen

Young Stevie hung around writer Joshua Rey, and declared, "One of these days I'm going to write the scariest book in the whole world. Excepting nobody would probably buy it." Sam gave him the ideas for Christine and kitchen knives. Stevie had a St. Bernard named Cujo. (BMAN)

King Thunder

A KISS-like rock group in the 1970s, they always wore makeup in public. Wildly popular, the group was performing before 80,000 fans when Sam leaped into the lead singer, Tonic. The band's last LP was called *Five All Night*. When they first came over from England in the 1950s, the band was known as The Dingles. (ROCK)

Kinman, Doc

Doctor in small Louisiana town where Sam found himself as sheriff. He couldn't determine the cause of death of Bart Aider, and had to have the Coroner from Shreveport come in. His son was Will Kinman. (TRILOGY)

Kinman, Willis Gunerson

Will Kinman was the son of the local doctor, and spoke with a stutter. He seemed to like Abagail Fuller, and eventually proposed to her. Sam leaped into Will the night before their wedding just after the pair had made love. Will was now 27 and deputy sheriff. Sam found himself falling for Abagail big time. He had picked up Will's stutter, but after they made love, he lost the stutter completely. Sam saved Abagail from a lynch mob and leaped. Will and Abagail never married. He moved out west to write a book. On the night Sam and Abagail made love, they conceived a daughter, Sammie Jo. (TRILOGY)

Klingman, Mrs.

She taught piano to Mac Ellroy's children, and showed an intense interest in purchasing a bomb shelter. She had survived the horrors of Dachau, and when Sam told her not to worry about a Soviet attack, she reminded him that she was told the same thing about the Germans. (NUCLEAR)

Knight, Pat

Tyler Means' old partner came riding into Coffin, Arizona just after Sam leaped into the old gunfighter. Knight declared he was the one who killed the Claggett boys, not Tyler. Okay, so he ambushed two of them and Tyler helped him kill the other two. Still, Tyler had been telling lies about the incident, and he was going to set the record straight with a gunfight. Knight killed his first man when he was fifteen, and was a crack shot, even when drunk. Sam asked him why he didn't stay around Coffin after the shoot-out, and he explained that he had gone out to tell the Claggetts' sister Ruthie and he just never came back. Sam outdrew Pat at the showdown but refused to shoot. After signing a TV deal on Tyler's behalf, Sam suggested to the network executive that there should be a place for Pat Knight as a consultant – just to make sure the tales are told straight. (GUN)

Kochifas, Nick

A shipping magnate who moved drugs, contraband and other shady items on his boats. Ziggy says he is going to get killed by a Colombian drug lord in 1976. In the meantime, he is going to kill Dana Barrenger, his former secretary, who testified against him in a trial. Sam changed history by killing Nick before he could get Dana. (CHARM)

Kramer, Doc

He knew that Roy Brown would be arrested if he came into town, so he supplied the Vietnam vet with the drugs he needed to control his seizures. He died two days before Sam leaped into Roy's buddy Henry Adams. (BEAST)

Ku Klux Klan

When Sam leaped into a KKK member, he was disgusted, telling Al their symbol stands for everything his parents taught him to fight against. (JUSTICE)

Kyle

The son of Frank Bianca's girlfriend, Laura, he witnessed the murder of pharmacist Phil Hartman. In the original history, he was murdered by Hartman's killers. He had a recurring nightmare after his own father was killed that someone was chasing him and trying to kill him. Kyle couldn't remember anything about the killer, except he had money in his shoes. Kyle wore a leg brace, and went on to win the 100 meters butterfly in the 1994 Special Olympics. Frank was going to teach him to swim, but after Sam suggested he enroll in classes in the Y, Kyle goes on to win the gold. (PERM)

L

LaBonte, Gilbert

Owner and operator of the LaBonte Sewing and Quilting Academy, a New Orleans brothel. Sam leaped in just as Gilbert was being surprised for his birthday by the ladies, leading to what had to be one of the most embarrassing leap-ins ever for Sam when Marsha felt him up. LaBonte was engaged to Marsha, the madam of the house, but he ended up marrying Paulette, a younger and prettier lady. (COMFORT)

LaBonte Sewing and Quilting Academy

Gilbert's great-grandfather started the school in the Civil War era as a cover for a brothel. By 1961, it was "the best damn cathouse in New Orleans". (COMFORT)

LaForge, Ellie

Lee Harvey Oswald/Sam tried to get her to join the Fair Play for Cuba Committee in New Orleans. (LHO)

LaMotta, Connie

Jimmy's sister-in-law. At first, she was against having Jimmy in the house because he was clumsy and she was afraid he would hurt Corey. After Sam saved Corey's life, she turned around and decided to let him stay. In fact, she was teaching Jimmy how to read a few years later when Sam leaped back into his life. Instead of the happy family he was expecting, he noted wryly that women's lib had hit suburbia. Connie was cooking awful TV dinners for the family, and wasn't keeping house the way she used to. Her excuse was that she needed all the extra time to teach Jimmy how to read, but in fact she was not who she appeared to be. Connie had been replaced by Alia, another time traveler. Her mission was to break up the family and send Jimmy back to the institution. (JIMMY, EVIL)

LaMotta, Corey

Jimmy's nephew. Sam administered CPR after he nearly drowned, saving his life. When Sam returned to the family two years later, Corey was thinking of running away because his parents were fighting all of the time. (JIMMY, EVIL)

LaMotta, Frank

Jimmy's older brother. He wanted to help mainstream Jimmy into society and got him a job at the docks where he worked. When Jimmy was fired, Frank also walked out. After Sam rescued Corey and pointed out Blue's dyslexia, they got their jobs back. When Sam leaped back two years later, Frank was seriously considering an affair with Shirley Constantine, his secretary. (JIMMY, EVIL)

LaMotta, Jimmy

Sam leaped into this retarded man in order to help him get mainstreamed. He had been out of the institution for two weeks, and his brother had lined up a job interview at the docks on Oakland where he worked. Sam found himself clumsy, and doing things he considered stupid. This may have been nerves, but it helped him fit in as Jimmy, who had the IQ of a twelve-year-old. (JIMMY)

Sam was elated to find himself back as Jimmy two years later and to find the man was doing great and had just been named Employee of the Month at the Oakland Docks. Originally, Connie and Frank lived happily ever after, Corey went on to Stanford, and Jimmy got his own place. But something was changing that situation. Connie and Frank were at each other's throats, and Al said they would break up and Jimmy blamed himself for it and was institutionalized three weeks after the divorce, never to get out. Corey was untraceable. Sam found out the reason when he touched Connie. (EVIL)

When Jimmy's personality took over during Sam's trip to Havenwell, he told the staff that he was a special person with a real job and that he wanted to build a space ship. (SHOCK)

LaPalma, Frankie (Francesco)

Sam leaped into this Mafia hit man right after Frankie had made love to Teresa Pacci in Don Geno's attic. Frankie was doing a "banga-banga" on Teresa against the orders of the Don. When Don Geno was about to kill Frankie, Ziggy attempted a retrieval. Sam leaped into the godfather and Frankie returned. Frankie didn't remember a thing, and still thought it was the moment he and Sam had first switched places. (DOUBLE)

LaPalma, Primo and Segundo

Frankie's brothers. Sam sent the two of them off to Buffalo to plug a 1,000 watt hair-dryer in at a house in order to fulfil Ziggy's instructions for a retrieval. (DOUBLE)

LaPalma, Tony

Frankie's father. He took a bullet for Don Geno once, and so is close to the godfather. (DOUBLE)

LeBaron, Helen

Former model turned agent. Sam described her as a "shark in nylons". Her agency was on the edge of bankruptcy, and she was feeding drugs to her model, Edie Landsdale, to keep her "up" all the time. Helen was also dating photographer Karl Granson, and was upset because Karl was seeing Edie. Edie wasn't the first client she had fed pills. In 1962 her top model, Yvonne Moncrief, almost died from an overdose, and when she recovered she left Helen and went to work for Eileen Ford. After Helen nearly killed Edie Landsdale, her agency probably went bankrupt. (STROBE)

LeJeune, Mark

He held a hurricane-watching party at his apartment, and was so drunk that, depending on which eye he was looking through, he saw either Sam or Archie Necaise. (HURRICANE)

Lake Arrowhead

Frank Bianca had a cabin there, and his girlfriend Laura and her son Kyle traveled there thinking they would be safe from a murderer. (PERM)

Landon's Department Store

Across the street from the WOF radio studios in Peoria. Sam cracked on the air that he had the Invisible Man in his studio, and asked what he liked best about being invisible. In his best Al voice he leered that it was being able to go into the girls' dressing-room at Landon's. The worst part was not being able to find his mouth to put his cigar in. But, Al rejoined, that was nothing compared to getting the Invisible Girl in the back seat of the car. (PEORIA)

Landsdale, Edie

Farm-girl turned New York high-fashion model. She got into modeling so she could get her dad a tractor, send her sister to college and become a vet herself. She felt lost in NY with no friends or family, but adopted a cat named Wooster and several other strays. Her agent Helen LeBaron was keeping her on drugs, and would eventually give her a deadly overdose. Her family has been in Cooperstown, Indiana for three generations, and she ended up going back home. (STROBE)

Langly, Peter

The FBI called Peter Langly one of its finest agents, but Sam learned otherwise when he found himself protecting Dana Barrenger from Nick Kochifas. Langly turned out to be in the pay of Kochifas and was setting up Dana's murder. (CHARM)

Laura

Girlfriend of Beverly Hills salon-owner Frank Bianca. She worked in a boutique somewhere in the area. Her son Kyle was a witness to a murder next door to the salon, and she refused to let him speak to the police. The reason was that in 1981 her husband witnessed a mob hit in New Jersey and later the mob gunned him down. She still feared for her and her son's lives. She and Kyle would have been killed had Sam not saved them, and she went on to start a support group for victims of violent crime. She and Frank also get married. (PERM)

Lawford, Peter

Dennis Boardman/Sam attended one of his famous beach bashes on April 8, 1960. (NORMA)

Lawrence College

A Catholic college in Marion, Ohio. Donna Elesee was studying there in 1972, when Sam leaped into Dr. Gerald Bryant. (CROSSED)

Lead Balloon

Sam put all he had on this 40–1 long shot in order to try to extricate Martin Ellroy from a pair of tough gamblers. The horse won. (TALE)

Lee, Robert Z. "Bobby"

A shady Chicago promoter who wanted to sign the Dovettes – Lynelle Walters in particular – to a contract. Eventually he ends up doing 20 years in prison for statutory rape of a thirteen-year-old girl. (SONG)

LeMaitre

Author of *The Primeval Atom*. It's the poetry of phsyics. (CROSSED)

Leola

When Dotty Billings took Billie Jean Crockett to the hospital the first time she went into labor, she left this customer in rollers with a color and perm job. Leola wouldn't let Dottie's helper Effie take the rollers out, so when Dotty returned Leola's hair had turned purple. (8½)

Levering, Clinton

Billy Beaumont picked this kid up from a shanty town in east St. Louis and taught him everything – except the exact proportions of each chemical he used to make rain. This was probably because he mixed it up differently every time. Beaumont told Clinton that wherever he was when he really made it rain, he was going to settle down and give his equipment to his apprentice. Sam kept Billy's pledge when he made it rain. (RAIN)

Lewis, Jerry Lee

The singer was set to appear in Montgomery, Alabama on June 24th, 1958. Sam used a poster for his appearance as inspiration for the Miss Deep South talent show. (SOUTH)

Liberty Ship

During the Second World War, steel was so scarce that the US Navy actually built ships from concrete. Very few were left, even in the 1950s, when Sam co-piloted an airplane through the Bermuda Triangle. He spotted one, and when he had the pilot look for it, the ship had vanished. (SHIP)

Lindhurst, Jane

After losing her husband, Jane left Cleveland to go to New York to pursue a singing career. Although she was pushing 50 she fell in love with Joe Thurlow, a 25-year-old actor who honestly loved her and cared about her singing career. Unfortunately, her son and his wife arrived for her 50th birthday to attempt to convince her to return to Cleveland. (Or, as Al put it, a fate worse than death.) Jane was very much into the '60s scene, wearing the hottest clothes and going on peace marches, much to the dismay of her conservative son. After Joe/Sam was offered the Boxer Boy job, he convinced the agency to take her on to sing the jingle. She never made it big, but she stayed in New York and she's happy. (PLAY)

Lindhurst, Neal and Liz

Jane Lindhurst's son and his pregnant wife. They came to New York from Cleveland to convince Jane to return home. (PLAY)

Lionel

Superintendent of the building in which Nick Allen had an office. In the original history he killed Allen, his partner Phil Grimsley and the newsboy Seymour in order to get to Allison Grimsley. He was deluded that she loved him. (SEYMOUR)

Lisa

Archie Necaise's ex-girlfriend couldn't let go of her old lover. Even though Sam evacuated her inland because of hurricane Camille, she returned, saying the roads were washed out, even though they weren't. After she had tried to kill Archie's current girlfriend Cissy Davis, she attempted to turn the knife on herself. She ended up spending a couple of years in intensive therapy and got her problems straightened out. (HURRICANE)

Lobelia

A weed-like flowering herb identified by blue and white flowers that are split down the middle. The petals contain chelidonic acid, which acts as a relaxant to suppress certain hormones produced in the brain. Sam boiled a quantity of the herb in an attempt to control Roy Brown's seizures. (BEAST)

Loggia, Vincent "Vinny the Viper"

A real slimy man with mob connnections, he tried to have Sam killed because he was interfering with his plans to marry Catherine Farlington, heir to Farlington Nautical. He also had pretensions of culture, badly misquoting the classics at every turn. He had a criminal record in New York. Still, to Weathers Farlington IV, his offer to buy out the family business was opportune, as they were quite strapped for cash. (BRIDE)

Loman, Bo

Clayton Fuller's deputy became sheriff on his death in 1955 and was still holding that position when Sam returned in 1966 and 1978. (TRILOGY)

LoNigro, Herkie

Played basketball with Sam at Elk Ridge. In the original history, he went on to be a mechanic at John Deere, but because Sam won the game he got a scholarship and became a doctor. (HOME)

LoNigro, Sebastian

Physics professor at MIT. In the summer of 1973, he and Sam worked out the string theory at his lake cabin in the Berkshires. When Sam was Peter Langly, an FBI agent assigned to protect Dana Barrenger, he took her to the cabin, assuming they would be safe. After it was all over, the professor arrived. "Don't you know who I am?" Sam shouted. "I'm Sam Be-"' Then he leaped. LoNigro and Dana Barrenger later married. (CHARM)

Lopez, Sgt. (US Marine Corps)

Gunnery Sergeant over Lee Harvey Oswald. He didn't like
Oswald's attitude and tried to beat him up in a bar.
Oswald may have killed him originally as Sam was there
to see that he wasn't killed. Lopez later saved the lives of
seventeen Marines and was given a posthumous Congressional Medal of Honor. Presumably he was KIA. (LHO)

Lorraine

Joey DeNardo's finacée. He left her in 1982 after witnessing a mob murder, and she set out to find him. They used
to perform together, and she was the lyricist when they
wrote songs. She went to find Joey at the instigation of her
new fiancée Carl Morgan, in order to convince herself that
it was indeed over. Morgan turned out to be Nick Bellini,
who had committed the murder Joey had witnessed.
(PIANO)

Lorrea, Tearsa Margaretta

At age 28, she worked as a prosecutor in the District
Attorney's office in Florida. She felt that Jesus Ortega was
innocent and risked her career to attempt to prove that.
For her trouble, the DA had her disbarred in 1972 for im-
moral conduct and she spent the rest of her life working in
a Florida unemployment office. She told Sam she watched
her boss manipulate the law and ignore the system and
become everything she has ever hated about lawyers. Al
decided she was okay, and was very surprised to see a
lawyer with morals. After Sam exposed the District Attorney's misdeeds, Tearsa stayed on and reopened four of the
cases he had pushed through court, and had two of them

overturned for insufficient evidence. As far as we know, she is still practicing law. (LAST)

Lothos

The artificial intelligence unit that controls Alia's assignments. There are some indications that this time travel project is set in the future, and may have built on Dr. Beckett's theories. The participants use terms such as "leaping" and "Swiss cheese", and the electric leap effect is essentially the same. Lothos, however, seems to have more control than Ziggy ever did. For example, he has the power to send his Leapers where he wants, and to reward and punish. He was not pleased with Alia's performance the first time she encountered Sam. He also has the power to pull a Leaper out at any time. Their Imaging Chamber is called the Holding Chamber. When Lothos sends out a Leaper, there is a 48-hour window in which he or she has to get home. After that, the percentage drops with each leap. Apparently he has "deep input" sessions with staffers. During one with Thames, the computer told him that sending Alia out was a mistake. It seems Lothos has some sort of master plan, but no one outside of the staff knows what it is. (EVIL, RETURN, REVENGE)

Lou

Owner of the Cocono Club, he fired Parker and MacKay after Mack MacKay physically went after a heckler. (STAND)

Lucille

Snuck off with Al at a Christmas party into the Energizing Chamber to exchange "Christmas gifts". (TESS)

M

McBain, Katie

Proving rape can be very difficult and traumatic to the victim, as Sam found out when he leaped into this teenager with the mission to prosecute the case. In this case it was date rape, as Katie had dated Kevin Wentworth a couple of times before. This time he made advances, and when she refused them he beat and raped her. The town was against Katie, branding her a "bad girl". Kevin's parents were very influential, and no one believed the teenager would do such a thing. After Al rigged the Imaging Chamber so Sam could hear Katie, he testified in the court trial, but Kevin was acquitted. When he tried to rape Katie again, Sam was still there and beat him up. (RAPED)

McBain, Jim

At first, Katie's father was very angry over his daughter's rape. He felt powerless to do anything. He had trouble supporting Katie in pressing charges, but eventually changed his mind and backed her decision. (RAPED)

McBain, Libby

Katie's sister thought it might be a good idea if the charges were dropped because of all of the stress being put on the family. At first she didn't believe her sister when she said she had been raped. (RAPED)

McBride, Diane

Sam found himself on a honeymoon with this woman, and his mission was to help her pass her bar exam. In the original history, the man who beat her out for the vacant seat left by her father's death (Senator Max Brown of Ohio) became the Committee chairman. He never believed Sam was traveling in time. Al proposed to prove it by changing a historical event, namely the Gary Powers U2 spy-plane mission. Sam was unable to do that, but did help Diane pass the bar exam. The result was that – as Al watched – she became the head of the Committee and granted funding for another year. She remarked to Al that she seemed to remember meeting a Samuel Beckett at some time, but couldn't remember when. "It'll probably come to me when I least expect it," she said. "Like in bed tonight." (HONEYMOON)

McBride, Tom, Lt. (NYPD)

When Sam leaped into Tom McBride, it was in the middle of a passionate kiss from his new wife as the "Honeymoon Express" pulled out of Manhattan for Niagara Falls. (HONEYMOON)

McCann, Billy

He and Emma Rickett were on the state championship speech team in dramatic interpretation in high school, and met again in 1964 while both were on family vacations. While Emma had to forego college to start a family, Billy had an astounding academic career, getting a Ph.D. at Northwestern where he then taught for seven years, then went on to Yale, Cornell and Berkeley. By 1966 he was widowed and had a daughter named Beth. Hank Rickett was afraid his wife may have still been harboring feelings for McCann. (RUNAWAY)

McCarty, Rod "the Bod"

Before he was a dancer he played football as an All-American split end for USC, but got sidelined by a knee injury. After that, he went touring with the Chippendales road company. Sam leaped into Rod just as he was being mobbed by a group of women. (DANCER)

McGill, Tess

Fiery tomboy cowgirl and heir to the 50,000 acre Riata spread in West Texas. Her widowed father Chance was pushing her to get married as Sam leaped into the vet, Doc Young. She decided she would challenge Doc to keep up with her for a week. If he could, she would marry him. (TESS)

McGrath, Flash

Member of the 1970s rock band King Thunder. He seemed rather anxious to be the star of the band, and was trying to get the leader, Tonic, to let the group play some of his songs. Sam briefly suspected him of plotting to kill Tonic. (ROCK)

McHorner, Alice

She used to live in the house Joshua Rey had in 1964. She lived there before she moved to Salem, and her spirit is said to still haunt the house. (BMAN)

McKnight, Tully

The local coventry handyman was fixing windows at Joshua Ray's house and told Sam that "Them that dance with the Devil are bound to get scorched." Then he declared, "What's time to Old Scratch? Yesterday's tomorrow to him." Sam just missed catching Tully as he fell to his death from a ladder. After the Boogieman incident, Al told Sam he was there to save Tully, but Sam knew what it was before Al finished telling him and raced up the stairs to save Tully from a bad trip. (BMAN)

MacKay, Macklyn (Mack)

Half of the comic duo of Parker and MacKay. He was the half with the attitude. After Sam leaped into Parker, Mack got the act fired for being way too hard on a heckler. He was going to vanish after the debut of Parker, MacKay and Washarski in Las Vegas in the original history. His body was found in 1982. And 1985. And 1989. Sam had to convince Mack to let Frankie Washarsk join the team, and later on got him to admit that yes, he really did love Frankie. She loved him, but the two were constantly at each other's throats. Also vying for Ms. Washarski's affections was Carlo DeGlorio, owner of the Las Vegas Golden Sand Hotel. DeGorio was about to bump off MacKay when Sam told him that the two comics were engaged, and that was why Mack was being so protective of her. DeGorio changed his tune and offered to pay for the wedding. Frankie and Mack did marry, and formed their own comedy team. (STAND)

MacKenzie, Charles Lee

"Oh my God, I'm Popeye!" Sam exclaimed to himself as he caught a glimpse in a store window as he disembarked from a bus. A little detective work told him his name, that he was an Aviation Machinist's Mate, 2nd Class, US Navy, that he had just shipped back from the Far East, and he was in Oak Creek Ohio, August 4, 1953. What he didn't know was that he was bringing back a surprise Charlie had written to his parents about – a Japanese bride named Machiko. (MACHIKO)

MacKenzie, Eileen

Charlie's sister died a little over a year before he returned from duty in Japan. She got pregnant, and Naomi says she was the only one who stood by her. Eileen drove her car off a bridge. The sheriff said it was an accident, but everyone believed it was really suicide. (MACHIKO)

MacKenzie, Henry

Charlie's dad reminded Sam of his own dad through his smile and his laugh. He had little trouble accepting Machiko. (MACHIKO)

MacKenzie, Lenore

Charlie's mother was totally against having Machiko in the house. She seemed to be very prejudiced, refusing

Machiko's gift of a kimono. After she and her daughter-in-law had an argument, Machiko ran away and was nearly killed. In the hospital, Sam asked her to go in and talk to her. Lenore couldn't, because she couldn't forgive her daughter Eileen. She did in her heart, but never to her daughter's face, and this pain was keeping her from forgiving Machiko. She felt she couldn't do for her what she couldn't do for her own daughter. When Sam and Machiko re-tied the knot in an American ceremony, however, Lenore entered wearing the kimono and bowed deeply. All was forgiven. (MACHIKO)

MacKenzie, Machiko

Japanese bride of Charlie MacKenzie. She had a tough time getting accepted by Charlie's family and friends, partly because of her nationality, and, in the case of Charlie's old girlfriend, out of jealousy. (MACHIKO)

Mad Dog

A member of the Cobras motorcycle gang who got his name from his temper. (REBEL)

Magnum, P.I.

Susan Bruckner was a big fan of the show and didn't want to miss it. But Sam told her not to worry, it would be on for another eight years. (ANOTHER)

Magnum, Thomas

Sam mentioned the fictional private detective to Seymour and Allison Grimsley. They had no idea who "Phil Allen" was talking about. (SEYMOUR)

Magrez

A star 54 light years from earth. It's the faintest star in the bowl of Ursa Major, and was "born" in the year 1945. (BACK)

Ma'Maw & D

An elderly couple riding out hurricane Camille at Unabelle's. They were celebrating their 64th wedding anniversary that day. (HURRICANE)

Mallard Correctional Facility for Women

Located in Mallard, Ohio, Sam and Alia found themselves here as inmates. (REVENGE)

Man of La Mancha, The

Sam leaped into a touring actor in the road show of this play in 1979. (CATCH)

Manny

The actor who played Sancho in *The Man of La Mancha* when Sam leaped into the road company. He had a thing for Michelle, who played Dulcinea. He had also betted heavily on horses. (CATCH)

Marchezak Dairy

Mike delivered milk for his family's dairy in Crown Point, Indiana. The dairy had been in business since 1927. (BACK)

Marchezak, Kelly

Ran the diner in Crown Point, Indiana. Her husband was Mike, the milkman. (BACK)

Marchezak, Mike

The milkman in Crown Point, Indiana. He and Tom Jarret were friends. He lost a leg in World War II. (BACK)

Mario

When this nightclub owner found out he had a deaf waitress working for him, he thought it would be a great gimmick to have Diana Quina as a deaf stripper. (DANCER)

Mario's Hideaway

This New York club was known for its exotic dancers, male and female. They also had a prostitution racket going on the side. (DANCER)

Mariska

A Russian woman (and most probably a spy) teaching Oswald Russian in Japan. (LHO)

Marlet, Karen

Left a widow when her husband John Burke was killed in Vietnam, she married Luke Marlet, one of his friends. She babied her son Daniel; probably being over protective was her way of making sure she didn't lose her son too. (BEAST)

Marlet, Lucas (Luke)

Sheriff's deputy who had served in Vietnam along with three of his high school buddies. Luke carried the psychological scars of an incident in which John Burke had been killed because Luke disobeyed a direct order to go inside a hooch and kill an old man. No one knew the hooch was booby trapped, and when Burke went inside it exploded in a mass of flames. After he returned home, he married John's widow, Karen, and never told her the real story surrounding her first husband's death. Karen knew, though, but it didn't matter to her. Once he got the incident off his chest and cleared things up with his remaining buddies, he and Karen went on to have two kids of their own. (BEAST)

Martha

Al spent the night with "this dish" after a championship basketball game that went into overtime. He was almost too late to help Sam pilot the X-2. (PILOT)

Martinez, Celia

Chuey's mother was never married, though she told her son that his father had died. She sneaked across the border to El Paso three days before giving birth, just so her son could be a US citizen. She, however, was not, and was being taken advantage of both by her employer and her landlord Ruben DeGuerra. She was three months and $800 behind in the rent, and Ruben suggested "another" way to pay the rent, but she refused. Chuey didn't know about the money problems until Ruben told him and suggested if he threw the game DeGuerra would call off the debt. Sam kept Chuey straight, and Celia married Manuel Vega, which made her a citizen. (ALL)

Martinez, Chuey

Hot running back for the Jaguars. He and his best friend, quarterback Eddie Vega, have made plans to get scholarships at the same school and study medicine. He would have thrown the championship game because Ruben DeGuerra, his family's landlord, told him to do so or he would throw his family out because they owed back rent. (ALL)

Martz, Tony

Track coach at Prescott Naval Academy. After admitting he was gay, he left the school and ended up coaching out west. (HONOR)

Masters, Ben

The sheriff in Coventry County, Maine was Joshua Ray's rival for Mary Greely. At least part of the time during Sam's leap he was the Boogieman. (BMAN)

Masters, Dr. Harvy

Staff member at Havenwell Hospital who was convinced Sam Beederman was suffering from Multiple Personality Disorder. (SHOCK)

Masterson

Guard at Mallory who was watching the box where Alia was shackled to the wall. (REVENGE)

Matsuda, Tamlyn

A psychic brought in by the San Francisco police in hopes of gaining a clue to a series of murders in Chinatown. When she looked at Dylan Powell/Sam in the mirror, she saw Sam's reflection instead of that of the reporter and recognised Sam as the man she had seen in a dream. He rescued her from death. Sam did keep her from being the next victim, and before he leaped she told him she knew it was time for him to go and that they would never see each other again. (EYES)

Meadows, Erwin, Major (USAF)

USAF intelligence officer assigned to Project Blue Book. He was skeptical about the whole thing, and was not pleased with Dr. Hardin's methods of obtaining information. (BRIGHT)

Means, Lucy

Working as a waitress in a restaurant/saloon, Tyler's daughter-in-law was having a tough time making ends meet. Her husband Peter had been killed in World War II. After Sam outdrew Pat Knight, preserving Tyler's reputation, he secured a TV deal that provided for the family. (GUN)

Means, Stevie

Tyler's grandson was always after the old man to let him handle the guns. He idolized his grandfather and believed every one of his tall tales. In the original history, after Tyler was killed Stevie's bubble burst and he ran away from home and turned to a life of crime, going in and out of jails for the rest of his life. When it looked like Sam wasn't going to face Pat Knight in a shoot-out, Stevie decided to defend the family honor himself and Knight wasn't about to stop him. (GUN)

Means, Tyler

Legend has it that this gunfighter cleaned up Coffin, Arizona almost single-handedly. In 1957 he was 82 years old and was participating in a daily re-enactment of the shoot-out in which he supposedly killed four Claggett Brothers. Tyler, or "T" as his family called him, had a reputation for telling tall tales, and in fact these stories had kept him in drinks for years. After his story was written up in *Reader's Digest*, his old partner Pat Knight arrived in town, calling Tyler a liar and asking for a shoot-out at high noon the next day. Tyler would have died in the shoot-out had Sam not been there instead of the old gunfighter. After Sam outdrew Knight, he secured a deal for a TV series about Tyler's life and got Knight signed on as consultant. (GUN)

Meyers, Clifton

As the warden at Mallard Correctional Facility for Women he felt a few perks came with the job, particularly his choice of the inmates. Meyers had planned to set up Elizabeth Tate in the murder of Carol Benning, one of his conquests who had died after a botched abortion. Zoey leaped into him in order to search for Alia, who had been traced there. From what little we know of his personality, they were probably a perfect fit. Zoey was anxious to see how "the other half" lived, and made plans to seduce inmate Liz Tate, not knowing she was Sam Beckett. (REVENGE)

Michaels, Dr.

Gave medical testimony concerning the death of Father Torelli at Julio Ortega's trial. Sam used his testimony to convince Tearsa that there must be an extra bullet lodged somewhere in the church. (LAST)

Michelle

She had the role of Dulcinea in *The Man of La Mancha*. She was attracted to Ray Hutton, but apparently it was not mutual. Michelle was very jealous of Nicole, and plotted to make Sam believe that Nicole was seeing John O'Malley, the star. In return for his compliance in the plot, Michelle gave herself to Manny after he'd been hitting up on her for years. (CATCH)

Midnight Marauder

Defender of the Faith. Protector of the Innocent. Okay, a dweeb named Arnold Watkins who ran around campus in a silly suit. Arnold had a death wish because of the guilt he had felt ever since his parents were murdered. (RETURN)

Miller, Julie

While her husband was in Vietnam she met another man. Asking for a divorce was difficult after all Ron had been through, but perhaps in a way it was easier because then she didn't have to deal with the realities of war. (NO-WHERE)

Miller, Ronald, Captain (US Marine Corps)

After serving two tours of duty in Vietnam, this 26-year-old soldier got his legs blown off by a land mine and was in a San Diego veterans' hospital for rehabilitation when Sam leaped in. The time traveler had the task of preventing the suicide of Miller's roommate Billy Johnson, who was paralyzed from the neck down. Secondarily, he had to try to save Miller's marriage to Julie because records showed his oldest son joined the Marines and saved his entire tank crew during the Gulf War. (NOWHERE)

Milo

The mascot for the Galveston Mustangs was a pig. Whoever performed the worst in the game had the "privilege" of taking care of Milo. (BALL)

Mintz, Dr. Timothy

Sam leaped into this Stanford University parapsychologist while he was investigating claims by Troian Claridge that her dead husband was calling to her. He was quite fond of Troian, as Al reported that in the Waiting Room the first thing he did was ask about her. (TROIAN)

Misfits, The

Sam saved Marilyn Monroe's life so she could make this, her last – and arguably best – film. (NORMA)

Miss Deep South

Sam found himself as a contestant in the 35th annual beauty contest featuring women from all over the region.

It was the biggest beauty contest in the south. Sam won the title. (SOUTH)

Miss Sugar Belle

Darlene Monty who won this beauty title and the right to compete in the Miss Deep South pageant. (SOUTH)

Mister Ed

Mac Ellroy's family was watching this program when a news bulletin broke in saying the US had intercepted a Soviet cargo ship, but had let it pass the blockade when no missiles were found on board. (NUCLEAR)

Mitral stenosis

The narrowing of the valves around the heart. Sam theorized a childhood bout with rheumatic fever may have caused this condition in Ronnie Sammis. (CHAMP)

Mole, Geoffrey

Real name of King Thunder's lead singer, Tonic. (ROCK)

Moments to Live

Sam leaped into this popular TV soap opera in the middle of a death scene. (MOMENTS)

Mongolians

The Battling Rooskies were supposed to wrestle this duo for the tag team championship, but the Mongolians got drunk in Denver, punched out two policemen and landed in jail for their trouble. The Shiloh Boys were put in their place on the card. (CHAMP)

Monroe, Marilyn

Sam leaped into this legendary movie star's driver on April 4, 1960, in order to make sure that she lived long enough to make *The Misfits*. In the original history, she died on April 8, most likely at Peter Lawford's house after taking Nembutal. Sam administered CPR after her pulse and breathing had stopped. Sometimes Marilyn just wanted to be plain Norma Jean, and after Sam called her a misfit, she had the movie renamed. Miss Monroe died in August of 1962 of an overdose of barbiturates and alcohol. (NORMA)

Montocelli, Rita and Rose

A pair of old maids whose sole purpose in life seemed to be nit-picking the priests at St. Dorothy's. Sam later borrowed their car to go after Father Mac. (FAITH)

Monte, Carlo

Carlo Monte and the Monte Carlo Nights played aboard the Queen Mary for the passengers' dancing pleasure. When Sam asked him in French to play a tango, Monte replied (sans accent) that he doesn't speak French. He just speaks with a French accent. (BRIDE)

Montgomery, Richard, Lt. (Confederate Army)

He wounded John Beckett in battle and chased him through the woods. Lt. Montgomery was also a suitor for Olivia Covington. (STATES)

Monty, Darlene

She had just won the title of Miss Sugar Belle and was leaving for the Miss Deep South pageant when Sam leaped into this beauty queen. In the original contest, Darlene placed third and used the money she won to go to med school and become one of the first female cardiologists in the country, so Sam couldn't blow the pageant for her. He had all kinds of trouble, such as when he appeared before the judges and balked at the Chastity Declaration, and during the talent show rehearsal when he was wearing a Carmen Miranda outfit and had to sing and dance 'Cuanda La Gusta'. When the pageant rolled around, he knew he couldn't perform that number, and out of desperation sat at the piano and belted out 'Great Balls of Fire'. The crowd went wild and Sam won.

Darlene was sharing a room with a girl named Connie, a.k.a. Miss Corn Muffin. Sam's other job was to keep Connie from ruining her life by having some revealing photographs taken somewhat against her will. (SOUTH)

Moody, Theodore Wallace

By pushing murder cases through the courts, this Florida District Attorney had furthered his political career and was now running for governor. Five men were on death watch because of his tactics. After Sam exposed Moody, his reputation went down the toilet. (LAST)

Morgan, Carl

Nick Bellini's pseudonym. (PIANO)

Morgan, Miss

Sam's Kindergarten teacher. They danced at his graduation. She married the principal that summer and he didn't get over it until he met Miss Sedlack – his first grade teacher. (TESS)

Mosnick, Sibby

Played basketball with Sam at Elk Ridge. In the original history he went on to be a bank teller, but after Sam won the game he got a scholarship and became a doctor. (HOME)

Mundy, Clyde

Elk Ridge Chief of Police in 1971. (LAND)

Multiple Personality Disorder

After Sam received an electroshock treatment and the personalities of people into whom he had leaped in the past began to assert themselves, Dr. Masters believed Sam was suffering from this disorder. He was fascinated that all of the "personality displacements" were in the future, and that and some imaginary person named Al was the only constant in each personality. (SHOCK)

Mustangs

Minor league baseball team in Galveston, Texas. Doc
Fuller/Sam pitched for them. (BALL)

'My Happiness'

Elvis Presley was to have sung this and 'That's When Your
Heartaches Begin' when he cut the record for his mother,
but Sam couldn't remember them so had to settle for 'Blue
Christmas'. (MEMPHIS)

Myers, Peg

Miss Deep South pageant director. She was also a former
Miss Orange Blossom, Miss Wisteria, and second runner-up in the Miss Praline pageant, which she would have
won if one of her batons hadn't failed to ignite. And of
course she was Miss Deep South of 1946. She taught Sam
how to walk like a lady. Sam learned she had once posed
nude for photographer Clint Beaumont, and he was black-
mailing her with the pictures so he could be the pageant
photographer and get at more girls. (SOUTH)

Myerwich, Chuckie

Young pitcher for the Galveston Mustangs. Chuckie was
hot, but he had a lot of anger inside of him and he drank a
lot. He reminded Sam of Al – angry, but Sam saw there a
good guy beneath the anger. In the original history,
Chuckie was caught with Bunny Twilly, daughter of the
team owner. Sam attempted to rescue him, and in the process was caught and they were both kicked off the team.
The owner reluctantly let them back on after several of the

Mexican players were picked up by Immigration. Sam learned that much of this man's anger stemmed from his father having abandoned him as a child. Sam managed to reunite the two in the end, and Chuckie went on to become a big league pitcher. (BALL)

Myrtle

She was the housekeeper in the Cotter household. When Sam asked her about what really happened between Delilah Barry and Houston Cotter, Myrtle told the truth as she knew it, but refused to swear on a Bible in court to tell the truth. (HELP)

N

Naomi

This "bottled brunette" used to be Charlie MacKenzie's girlfriend before he shipped out with the Navy. She waited for him, but wasn't exactly true. Furious that Charlie came home married, she tried everything she could think of to break the pair up. (MACHIKO)

National Motors Corporation

Detroit car company where Samantha Stormer and Gloria Collins worked. (GLORIA)

Necaise, Archie

Sam leaped into the new deputy sheriff in Jackson Point, Mississippi, just as hurricane Camille was about to strike. His job was to keep Archie's girlfriend Cissy Davis from being killed by the hurricane, while still evacuating a hurricane party as the deputy had done in the original history. Sam managed both. (HURRICANE)

Nevsky, Valerie

She worked at Mario's Hideaway, possibly as a partner in the business, but her real business was setting the waitresses up for "dates'. She would be arrested for prostitution in 1977. (DANCER)

Nicole

Sam's piano teacher when he was fifteen, he met her again about a decade later when he leaped into Ray Hutton. Ray and Nicole had had a relationship at Juliard (where she left Elk Ridge to go), but they went their separate ways career-wise afterward. She was in Syracuse in 1979 when she auditioned for the understudy to Dulcinea in *The Man of La Mancha*. She had been there ever since *Grease* had folded, not wanting to go back to New York and face the increasingly younger competition. Instead, she went back to teaching piano. While she didn't remember Sam Beckett directly, she did recall that one of her students warmed-up at the piano in exactly the same manner as Sam/Ray did. Sam fell for Nicole all over again, and apparently the earth moved for them one night. Despite the efforts of others in their company to part the pair, Sam declared his love for Nicole, and she her love for Ray. (CATCH)

O

O'Connor Cab Company

Max Greenman/Sam worked for this company located at 121 E. 55th Street in Manhattan. (WONDERFUL)

O'Connor, Frank

Owner of O'Connor Cab Company. He had offered a contest to his employees. The first driver to get $30,000 in fares in a one-year period would get his own medallion. The contest was nearly impossible to win, but Max Greenman was only $50 short with one day to go. Not wanting to give away the medallion, Frank set up Max's robbery. Sam discovered the plot after the robbery had taken place, and as part of O'Connor's probation deal he had to give the medallion to Max. (WONDERFUL)

O'Hare, Bunny

Her real name is Thelma Lou Dickey, but she worked at the Girls A–Go-Go Lounge as a stripper under the name of Bunny O'Hare. She seemed to be a pathological liar, telling Sam first one story and then another. First she told

Sam leaps into Nick Allen, a cheap detective in an expensive suit, arrested for a murder he didn't commit. *(Play It Again, Seymour)*

Sam is Shane "Funny Bone" Thomas, a leather-clad biker who, to prevent a murder, must ask Jack Kerouac for help. *(Rebel Without A Clue)*

Sam leaps into Darlene Monty, a beauty pageant contestant faced with preventing a fellow competitor's nude poses for a sleazebag photographer. *(Miss Deep South)*

Sam and Al dance a hilarious Carmen Miranda number together! *(Miss Deep South)*

Sam finds himself in the muck and mire of a pig sty as Patrick Young,
the local veterinarian who helps Buddy Holly compose . . . "Piggy Sue."
(How The Tess Was Won)

Sam is Herbert (Magic) Williams, a black Navy Seal in Vietnam. Sam finds himself in action with his brother Tom, one day before Tom is due to be killed. *(Vietnam – The Leap Home, Part II)*

In a poignant episode, Sam leaps home to Indiana and back into his family. *(The Leap Home, Part I)*

Sam is Victor Panzini, a member of a family trapeze act who must
reconcile the group's father and son whilst swinging in tight lycra!
(Leaping Without A Net)

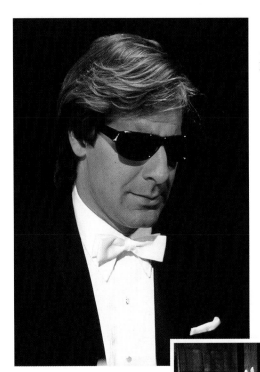

Sam has leaped into Andrew Ross, a blind concert pianist at Carnegie Hall who must prevent the murder of his assistant Michele. *(Blind Faith)*

Sam leaps into the coffin of an artist who lives as a vampire . . on the night of a ritual female sacrifice. *(Blood Moon)*

Sam leaps into a mentally retarded adult and tries to fight the prejudice surrounding him and get him a job. *(Jimmy)*

In the "present" Al has to make the case for supporting the Project to Congress, or funds will be cut and Sam will be lost forever jumping through time. *(Honeymoon Express)*

Scott Bakula received a
Golden Globe Award for
Best Performance by an
Actor in a Television Series
Drama as Sam Beckett.

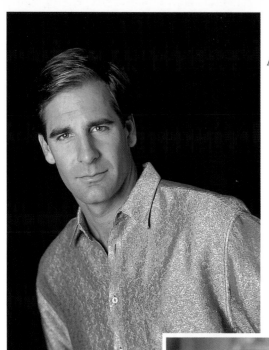

Dean Stockwell received a
Golden Globe as Best
Supporting Actor for his
portrayal of the
wisecracking Al.

Sam that she was really the mother of Christie Dalton, then admitted that she only told that story because she didn't think Buster/Sam would help her take the baby and return her to her real mother. Bunny said the baby's father beat her, and she didn't want the baby to suffer that same fate. She even lied about her age. But she was telling the truth about Christie's real mother, and Sam helped her return the baby. (MAYBE)

O'Malley, John

This brilliant, albeit drunken, theater actor was playing the lead in *The Man of La Mancha* in Syracuse when Sam leaped into the role of his understudy. He would literally break a leg – and his hip – at a benefit performance in three days unless Sam prevented the mishap. O'Malley played Don Quixote 763 times before he took his fall. (CATCH)

O'Reilly, Charlie

One of Michael Blake's childhood chums, he was laid off from Henderson's Bakery after Blake bought it and automated it. Finally he got drunk and jumped in front of a bus. (MIRACLE)

O'Reilly, Gordon

Sam found he was the third bounty hunter to attempt to bring in Diane Frost, a woman wanted for embezzling. His prisoner was not about to be taken in, and tried every trick in the book (and then some) to escape her captor. Originally, she shot Gordon and then was killed in making her escape. (HUNT)

O'Shannon, Pete, Sgt. (NYPD)

This mounted officer lived across the hall from Andrew Ross. His horse was named Daisy. He seemed a nice enough guy, feeding peanuts to Chopin and to the kids on his beat. But he was the man who had strangled three women in Central Park, and nearly got Michelle Stevens. (BLIND)

Oakland Docks

Where Jimmy and Frank LaMotta worked. (JIMMY, EVIL)

Omm

In 1969, as a cop working undercover as a guru, Sam gave this mantra to a group of hippies in San Diego. (MIA)

Operation Lazarus

A top secret mission the Bravo S.E.A.L. unit was going to undertake. Ten kilometers upriver from camp was a place called Ma Choi, where several American POWs were held. Their mission was to rescue the men. A guerrilla woman who was guiding them was actually leading them into a trap, which Sam detected. (NAM)

Ortega, Jesus

In one of his most dramatic leaps, Sam found himself being strapped into the electric chair to die for the murder of Father Vincent Torelli. Just as the switch was to be pulled, the governor phoned in a 48-hour reprieve. Ortega was an illiterate Cuban, but he managed to write out his own appeal, saying that crucial evidence was omitted from his trial. Helping him was Tearsa Lorrea, a prosecutor with the DA's office who was convinced of Ortega's innocence. In reality, Ortega had commited the crime, but his friend Raul Casta – also sentenced to die for the crime – was not even present when the murder was committed. Sam confessed that Ortega had acted alone and Casta went free. Sam leaped just as the switch to electrocute him was being pulled. (LAST)

Oswald, Lee Harvey

Widely believed to be the assassin of president John F. Kennedy in 1963. Sam leaped into his life at several points. Oswald used the name Alik in the Soviet Union, and that's what Marina called him. In the Marines he was a PFC, serial $ 1653230SN. His nickname in the Marines was "Ozzie Rabbit". (LHO)

Oswald, Marina

Met the man she called Alik in the Soviet Union where they married before he returned to the United States. Sam leaped in to Oswald as she was about to snap the infamous "rifle picture". (LHO)

Otto

The center for the Jaguars. Big guy. He looked in the mirror in the locker room and asked Chuey if he thought he looked like Elvis. And Chuey thought no, *he* did. (ALL)

Another man named Otto worked the bar at Mario's Hideaway. (DANCER)

Owens, Rodney

Diane Frost's boss. (HUNT)

P

Pacci, Teresa

Beautician who had been having an affair with Don Geno Prascotti. She broke off the affair, but Don Geno said it wasn't over yet, and any man who so much as looked at her would be rubbed out. She fell in love with Frankie LaPalma when she saw him standing in front of Luigi's Fish Market with a big .45 in his hand, blowing holes in the Giocanni brothers. When he spotted her hiding behind the salted cod and winked, she knew it was Kismet. They've "made it" in such diverse places as under a table at the Sons of Italy, beneath the West End and behind the furnace at St. Francis. Evenually, with the blessing of Don Geno/Sam, she and Frankie got engaged. (DOUBLE)

Pain in the Buffalo

Vanessa Foster's Indian Guide name, presumably foisted on her by her fellow campers. (SHREW)

Palermo, Tonchi

A miner in Cokeburg, PA who Sam saw as Frank LaMotta. Tonchi had a retarded brother who also worked at the mine. The two were trapped in the mine after an explosion. (MIRROR)

Palermo, Pete

Tonchi's mentally retarded brother. He looked like Jimmy LaMotta to Sam. (MIRROR)

Panzini, Eva

Eighteen-year-old sister of Victor and now star of the Flying Panzinis. She would die attempting the triple unless Sam was able to catch her. (NET)

Panzini, Laszlo

The patriarch of the Flying Panzinis, who were once the most famous aerial act in the world. After his wife Maria died in 1957 while attempting the triple, he reduced the act to simple routines and the Panzinis ended up playing small road shows. He's a proud man, and refused to admit the torn rotator cuff in his right arm was hindering his ability to catch. But he no longer let his son Victor perform because he was catching the night Maria died. Everyone knew she had a cold and shouldn't have been performing because her balance was off, but Laszlo found it easier to blame his son. (NET)

Panzini, Victor

Sam leaped, er, flew into the most famous circus act in the world on November 18, 1958. The family was once the star attraction at the Circus Vargas, until Victor's mother, Maria, died while attempting the triple without a net in Chicago. Since then Victor's father, Laszlo, has refused to let his son perform, blaming him for the accident. Victor was reduced to working as the safety man in the act, and it was up to Sam to get Victor flying again so he could catch his sister Eva when she attempted the triple in two days' time. (NET)

Pard

Buddy Holly's dog. Sam had no idea who the kid was, and tried to call him Pard, which normally would have worked under the circumstances in Texas. But every time he did, the dog barked. (TESS)

Park Grove Hotel

Diana Quina let herself get talked into meeting a "date" there in room 1203. If Sam hadn't stopped her, that one date would have started a string of events leading to her death from AIDS in 1986. (DANCER)

Parker, Davey

As the singing half of a comedy team (sort of like Dean Martin to Jerry Lewis), Sam had to keep the act together and keep the other half of the team alive. (STAND)

Parson, Lisa

A cheerleader who was sweet on Sam Beckett in 1969. "No Nose" Pruitt of Bentleyville had the hots for her, but she asked Sam to the post-game dance. In the original history, she married Pruitt in 1970, and they divorced after having two children. In the changed history she didn't marry Pruitt, but it's not said what became of her. (HOME)

Parsons, Bo

The prosecuting attorney in the case of Lila Barry. He had made a bargain with Leonard Dancey to reduce the charges if she would plead guilty, but Sam made Lila plead innocent, forcing Bo to ask for the chair. (HELP)

Patience

A girl Tyler Means and Pat Knight almost came to draws over in the old days. (GUN)

Paula

One of the three girls who made up The Dovettes. (SONG)

Peach Hill Home for the Mentally Ill

Laura Fuller had been committed there in 1953, but ended up staying there of her own accord. (TRILOGY)

Pearson, Reginald

There could be worse times to leap into a gentleman's valet, but Sam might be hard pressed to think of one after leaping into Michael Blake's "man" just as the billionaire was being helped into his underwear. That is, until Ziggy mentioned Sam might actually have to bathe Blake. (MIRACLE)

Peeping George

Samantha and Gloria's neighbor. The girls liked to give him a thrill once in a while. (GLORIA)

Phenytoin

The drug used to control Ray Brown's seizures. (BEAST)

Phillips, Dewey

The Memphis DJ who first played Elvis Presley's music on the air. (MEMPHIS)

Phillips, Mr.

The head of Sun Records. Sam had to convince him to give Elvis Presley an audition. (MEMPHIS)

Pierce, Stan and Lisa

An elderly couple who had a farm a couple of miles down the road from the Becketts. They've been in the area for 54 years, having moved there the year after they got married. Lisa remembered the time when Stan was away and John Beckett drove her to the hospital and waited for an hour with her. She said everyone knew the Beckett family. (LAND)

Piernic and Macovic

Honey nut cake and poppy-seed jelly-roll cake. These are traditional Polish Christmas foods. (MIRACLE)

Piggy

The name Sam gave to the pig he was treating in *How the Tess Was Won*. It was a girl pig, as Al so deftly pointed out, so perhaps the name was a reference to the Muppet Miss Piggy. (TESS)

Pilcher, Hank

Norma Jean's husband met his future wife when they were both in church – she was cleaning it and he was robbing it. He was unable to father a child, but wanted his wife to be a mother, so he went along with her plan to kidnap soap opera star Kyle Hart and seduce him. Hank was later convicted of kidnapping and assault and served six years, after which he opened a fixit shop next to the hospital where Norma Jean had been committed. (MOMENTS)

Pilcher, Norma Jean Bates

She flooded a detergent contest with entries so she could win a lunch with soap opera hunk Kyle Hart. The only problem was that she had the actor hopelessly confused with the role, and she and her husband Hank kidnapped Hart/Sam in order to have him father a child for her. Norma Jean was a paranoid with tendencies toward delusions and violence and had spent some time in a mental hospital. Sam tried to bring her back to reality by having Hank fake a heart attack, then insisting he had to operate, just like on TV. She got sent back to a mental hospital for several years. (MOMENTS)

Pistano, Francis (Frank) Guiseppe, Fr.

Sam leaped into this Italian-American priest in 1963. Father Frank was two years out of the seminary, and St. Dorothy's in Philadelphia was his first assignment. (FAITH)

Polly's Diner

Sam and Lorraine sought refuge there while running from Nick Bellini. It was called Polly's, but a lady named Thelma owned it. (PIANO)

Pompano Palace

A hotel right on the beach. Tell 'em Al Calavicci sent you, and they'll treat you first class. (TALE)

Poppa Dee

He was definitely against Ray Harper's relationship with Susan Brewster, and tried to beat a little sense into Ray at one point. When the Watts Riots boiled, he got shot in the femoral artery and died before he could be taken to a hospital. (B&W)

Porter, Rachel

Owner and General Manager of WOF radio in Peoria. Her father started the station, and she continued to carry on his dream of having the number one station. Her belief was they would achieve it through rock and roll, but certain townspeople saw it otherwise. (PEORIA)

Powell, Dylan

For some reason, this reporter at an independent TV station in San Francisco was getting anonymous tips in advance of a series of killings in Chinatown. At 59 years old, he was a month from retirement. Although he had been covering the city beat for a quarter century, his career had been going downhill until the murders. (EYES)

Prascotti, Don Geno

The Mafia godfather in Brooklyn. Frankie LaPalma was "a bingo, bango, bongo-ing" Teresa, and Don Geno wanted to kill (or maybe just castrate) him/Sam for it. When he finally confronted Sam and Teresa in his attic, Ziggy tried a retrieval program that ultimately resulted in Sam, he and the don switching places. Sam had Father Sebastian formally announce the banns of marriage for Frankie and Teresa at a bingo game. A little unorthodox, but Sam wasn't about to take any chances. So why hadn't he leaped? He had to help Nona win at Bingo. Don Geno would get knocked off by the Carlucci brothers the next April. (DOUBLE)

Prescott Naval Academy

A prep school located just outside of Lakeside, Michigan. (HONOR)

Presley, Elvis

Sam leaped into The King two days before he was to be discovered by Colonel Parker. He was there to help Sue Anne Winters, a local girl who was about to marry an old-fashioned southern gentleman. While Sam helped Sue Anne onstage at a talent show, he managed to turn the two of them into the next Donny and Marie. Sam's persistence paid off, and he got an audition with Sun Records and got Elvis's career back on track. (MEMPHIS)

Presley, Gladys

Elvis's mother didn't think he would make it as a singer, and admonished him to be realistic. (MEMPHIS)

Primeval Atom, The

By LeMaitre. Sam called it the poetry of physics. He quotes this passage to Donna: "Then came the explosion, followed by the filling of the Heavens with smoke. We've come too late to do no more than visualize the splendor of Creation's birthday." (CROSSED)

Process Schizophrenia

Sam suspected Phillip Stilbart suffered from this disease, in which a person's sense of self is slow in developing. The personality is incomplete, so the person has to fill up what's missing by imitating something they see or know. An example would be Hinkley watching *Taxi Driver* and identifying with the man who stalked the political candidate. (ROCK)

Project Blue Book

A classified government project investigating UFO phenomena. Sam found himself being interviewed by two of their operatives after he leaped into an elderly man who had seen a UFO. (BRIGHT)

Project Quantum Leap

A time travel experiment that "went a little ca-ca". PQL was Sam's brainchild, and he holds the key to his return. The Project cost 43 billion dollars and takes 2.4 billion per year to keep it going. (HONEYMOON)

The project itself is located at Stallions's Gate, New Mexico, presumably near the larger town of Stallion Springs, where Sam keeps a Post Office box (LHO). It must be somewhere just outside of Estiny, as Al pointed to the mountains and told Sam that PQL would be 30 miles in that direction in another seven years. They used cards for access until they got implants (ROBERTO). The site was also mentioned as being where the first atomic bomb was set off, so Los Alamos must be in the vicinity (PILOT).

Early on the government tried to shut the Project down because they thought it was too dangerous. Sam and Al believed in their work and managed to keep the Project alive. The place is outfitted with an operating room, where Billie Jean Crockett was placed when she went into labor. (8½)

The Waiting Room and Imaging Chamber are situated ten levels below ground in a cavern. (KILLIN, PILOT)

PQL has a Code 1 clearance. (KILLIN)

Sam told Carol Pruitt he created PQL in 1995. (KILLIN)

What is it like in the future? The style for the second half of this decade seems to lean toward dresses and accessories that light up. Special lanes are reserved for electromagnetic vehicles by the year 1999, and some appliances will be voice activated. (PILOT, BACK, KILLIN)

Pronti, Joey

A half-orphan whose father killed himself and mother took to the bottle and the streets. He and his older brother Tony scraped along together in Philadelphia. Joey was basically a good kid, although his brother committed a robbery and murder. When Tony went to prison, Father Mac saw to the boy's welfare. (FAITH)

Pronti, Tony

Joey's older brother was turning into a hardened criminal. Joey said he didn't use to be that way, but it was only after his father died that he turned angry and mean. In July of 1963 he robbed a store in which the clerk was killed. He did away with one of the witnesses, a twelve-year-old boy. Next he tried to kill the other witness, Father Mac of St. Dorothy's Chruch. He ended up doing serious time for his crime, but did straighten his life out once he got out of prison. (FAITH)

Pruitt, Becky

Carol's daughter. After Gooshie informed Sam she would be killed when the sheriff stormed the house, Sam released her. (KILLIN)

Pruitt, Carol

While held hostage by Leon Styles, Sam convinced her that he was not the serial killer, and proved it by his knowledge of medicine. Carol was a med student who had put her husband through college, and he left after he got what he wanted. While she still wasn't completely convinced that Sam was from the future, she did keep the sheriff from killing him. (KILLIN)

Pruitt, "No Nose"

This 6' 4" high school basketball player lost the tip of his nose in a reaping accident, and gained a nickname. He played for Bentleyville, and was the one person Sam had to beat on the court in order to help Elk Ridge win the game. (HOME)

Psychosynergize

Al's term for what happens when Sam's mind becomes intermingled with the person who he has changed places with. The best example of that was when Sam leaped into Oswald. (BRIGHT)

Ptah-Hotep II

Egyptian pharaoh believed to be of the 18th dynasty about 3500 years ago. His tomb was discovered by Drs. Dale Conway and Ginny Wills. The two never reported their discovery, though, as their 1957 expedition vanished without a trace. Keller and Hoskins discovered a papyrus in 1963 saying that Ptah-Hotep had a sarcophagus of solid gold. Legend has it he had a diamond scarab the size of a cow's eye called The Heart of Ptah-Hotep. With this he could work magic. The pharaoh's Ka is said to be inhabiting the burial chamber. Normally a false door is built for the Ka to pass through, but this time the false door turned out to be a cover for the real door to the burial chamber. (CURSE)

Pullbrook, Dr.

Marilyn Monroe's physician was called after she had suffered an apparent drug overdose at Peter Lawford's house. (NORMA)

Q

Quan, Major

The Vietcong officer who was holding Al and two other POWs at Ma Choi. (NAM)

Quantum Leaping, Laws of

When Sam leaps, he physically trades places with a person at some point in his lifetime. This is governed by the String Theory, detailed elsewhere. The other person, called the visitor, lands in the Waiting Room at Project Quantum Leap. (See Waiting Room)

In order for Al and Ziggy to get a lock on Sam, a person has to be in the Waiting Room. Otherwise, they have to use a nano-second search which could take over a month. (MIRROR)

People generally see Sam as the person into whom he has leaped, because the illusion of the physical aura stays behind. Conversely, people at PQL see the visitor as Sam.

In order to see what he looks like, Sam must look in a mirror. Apparently when he looks directly at himself, he sees himself, for when he leaped into Tonic, he had to place his hand over a mirrored surface to see the webbing in the fingers (ROCK). On the other hand, when he leaped into Bingo he found himself on the beach and a woman's bra in his hand. He looked down at his chest, as if looking for confirmation (LISA).

As with Al (see Hologram, Neuro), children under five and most animals can see Sam. Children exist in a natural alpha state, and because they and animals are pure of heart, they can see the truth (MOTHER, TALE, JUSTICE, PILOT). Some people with mental problems can also see Sam as himself, and so can angels, if you believe Angela (WONDERFUL). Psychic Tamlyn Matsuda could see Sam's reflection in the mirror, but could not see Sam as himself when she looked at him directly (EYES).

During the early leaps, Al could only see the illusion of the physical aura of the person into whom Sam had leaped. This caused some real problems when Sam leaped into Samantha Stormer, because Al found himself falling in love with his best friend (GLORIA). Perhaps that drove the project to find a way for Al to see Sam as Sam and the people in the Waiting Room as themselves (SOUTH, POOL). This modification came in especially handy when Sam leaped into a legless veteran. Al was able to warn Sam before he gave the game away (NOWHERE).

The illusion of the physical aura covers not only the appearance of the person, but his or her voice and weight (SONG, WRONG). When Sam leaps, the clothing also stays behind, so he's dressed in whatever the person would be wearing. And, of course, the people in the Waiting Room wear a Fermi Suit.

Sam generally carries his own physical strength and other characteristics. As Dr. Ruth Westheimer, for example, he ran over the tops of taxi cabs in New York City and beat up a man much larger than his host (RUTH). Sam could see perfectly when he leaped into blind pianist Andrew Ross, and could walk even though he had leaped into a man with no legs (BLIND, NO-WHERE).

Perhaps this is most aggravating when Sam leaps into a woman, because he has to remember not to walk like a man. He did use it to his advantage as Samantha Stormer when he got even with Buddy Wright. (GLORIA)

The most confusing body incident took place when Sam leaped into a sixteen-year-old pregnant girl. Sam experienced all of the classic symptoms of pregnancy – cravings, sickness, frequent urination, but Al insisted the baby was back at the Project with the mother. Still, Sam insisted he was pregnant. He felt the baby kick. As Sam lay on the delivery table in the last stage of labor, the baby vanished from the mother back in the Waiting Room, and the doctor with Sam said he could see the baby's head. Sam then leaped, avoiding becoming the first man to give birth to a child. (8½)

If there were any doubts that Sam's entire body leaped, they were permanently erased after he fathered Sammie Jo Fuller. (TRILOGY)

Sometimes certain characteristics of the person stay behind. Often this helps Sam in his mission, but it can also be a hindrance. As Lee Harvey Oswald, his mind kept melding with that of the assassin. Sometimes Oswald completely took over, and Sam did things he normally would not have done (LHO). Lawyer Larry Stanton's heart condition was left behind, causing a hindrance (TRILOGY). As Dr. Ruth, Sam found himself slipping into the mannerisms and accent of the famous sex therapist. Unlike Lee Harvey Oswald, however, these slips were often amusing and helped Sam complete his task (RUTH).

Sam created a set of basic rules for time travelers to follow. First and foremost, the time traveler is not allowed to change his or her own history. Sam tried once to alter his past with Donna Elesee, and it appeared not to have worked, as we don't know for sure if Sam had simply forgotten his marriage. Once again Sam had the opportunity to change his own history when he leaped into his sixteen-year-old self. He was only there to win a basketball game, but tried unsuccessfully to change other aspects of his past as well. His next leap was into his brother's S.E.A.L. unit in Vietnam, and he did get to save Tom's life. (CROSSED, HOME)

The rule prohibiting Sam to change the past to benefit himself personally in the future caused real problems when Sam, as Marty Ellroy, tried to bet on a horse race. Ziggy interpreted his actions as trying to affect his own future instead of Ellroy's and refused to give Al the results of the race. (TALE)

Al tried to change his own past when Sam leaped into San Diego in 1969. Rather than tell Sam what he was really there to do, he tried to get Sam to stop Beth from marrying Dirk Simon. Sam later had the opportunity to right that wrong. (MIA)

Sam also cannot tell anyone who he really is, as it may affect the chances of his leaping out. Still, he has told several people his true identity because it seemed to be the only way to accomplish his task.

Usually Sam leaps when he has accomplished his task, although sometimes he gets a little extra time. Originally they thought that if he failed he wouldn't be able to leap, but now they don't think that's the case. Sam cannot leap if the visitor is not in the Waiting Room. The most dramatic example of this rule was when Sam leaped into killer Leon Styles. (KILLIN)

Sam and Al once simo-leaped under one of two conditions needed to make it possible. The first would have been a lightning strike, which happened the instant Sam received a crucial dose of shock therapy at Havenwell. The other would have required the two of them to have been at ground zero during a nuclear explosion. Curiously, the latter is one of the ideas Ziggy had early on for getting Sam back to his own time. Sam and Al switched libidos as well as physical places, which led to some interesting consequences. (BACK, PILOT)

Sam and Alia found that if they held each other at the appropriate time, they were able to leap together. Alia was lost to Lothos, and two people arrived in the Waiting Room. (RETURN, REVENGE)

Hypnosis can alter the brainwaves so the observer might not be able to make contact. (REVENGE)

Since Sam leaps back and forth in time to seemingly random events, times of year rarely coincide. Christmas for him was July back at the Project, for example. (MIRACLE)

Quark

A microparticle of a proton or neutron, it's one of the smallest particles known to physicists. (SHOCK)

Queen Mary

The luxury cruise liner was to be the site of Catherine Farlington's wedding to Vincent Loggia. (BRIDE)

Quina, Diana

Sam found her working as a waitress at Mario's Hideaway, but for her that was just a stepping stone to a career as a dancer. Mario wanted to start her out as an exotic dancer (read "prostitute"), but when that happened in the original history, she died of AIDS in 1986. After Diana "ignored" a customer and the bartender, Sam realized she was deaf. Diana had left the Cheyenne School for the Deaf during her senior year. She had been there since the age of seven, after a car wreck which claimed her parents' lives and in which she sustained head injuries which made her deaf. Now she had come to New York, and was living in an old VW bus parked on the street. Sam took her to audition for Joanna Chapman, who ran one of the best modern dance companies around. It took two auditions and quite a bit of convincing, but Chapman eventually hired her. Diana became the lead dancer in three years, and eventually finished high school. (DANCER)

R

Race Car

Code name for the U-2 spy plane. (LHO)

Rafaella

The Bruckners' baby-sitter. (MOTHER)

Rain, how to make:

Use silver iodide, hydrochloric acid and acetone. The mixture is very unstable. Since the acetone makes the rest of the solution evaporate, it has to be launched immediately. In 1957 they used oatmeal boxes carried aloft by helium balloons. Sam added a picnic to the recipe. After all, it always rains when you try to have a picnic. (RAIN)

Rawlins, Jake

Sam leaped into this undercover detective for the San Diego Police Department on April 1, 1969 as he was working a bust disguised as a hooker. His real mission was to keep Jake's partner, Sgt. Robert Skaggs, from being gunned down. Instead, Al told Sam he was there to stop a woman named Beth from making the mistake of her life by marrying a lawyer named Dirk Simon. What he neglected to tell Sam was that Beth's M.I.A. (Missing In Action) husband was actually named Al Calavicci. Al was so hung up in trying to fix his own life that Sam nearly didn't find out about Skaggs until it was too late. (MIA)

Retrieval Program

This is the part of Project that really went ca-ca, leaving Sam stranded in time. Ziggy first tried to retrieve Sam after he had been Tom Stratton for 24 hours (PILOT). He tried again during a subsequent leap but it only resulted in Sam switching places with mob boss Don Geno in order to complete his task. Ziggy was 97.3% sure he could get Sam back, but only if he followed the computer's instructions to the letter: 1) At 22.15 GMT, plug in a 1,000 watt hair-dryer at a house located at 111 Erie Drive in Buffalo, NY; 2) At the designated retrieval time (22.28 GMT) Sam must be at the same location he arrived at; and 3) He must dupli-cate the event that was occurring when he arrived. The hair-dryer blew a pole transformer and started the great blackout of the eastern seaboard. (DOUBLE)

When Sam ended up in his own time after he and Al simo-leaped, he proclaimed that his mind must have been working on all this in the background the entire time and proceeded to adjust the software so they could hit the bullseye. This was necessary in order for Sam to leap into Al's precise position in 1945, and was also used later when Bingo was sent back to the evening of Marci Riker's death to prevent the event. When Sam stepped into the Acceler-ator to swap places with Al, the odds of him coming back were only 9.6%. The new data also suggests that the very first leap was pretty much random. (BACK, LISA)

Rey, Joshua

A sort of second-rate H.P. Lovecraft who lived and wrote in Coventry, Maine. Joshua was engaged to Mary Greely, his part-time research assistant. He had kind of a creepy house that dated back to before the Salem witch trials and was said to be haunted by a previous occupant who had been burned in Salem as a witch. (BMAN)

Reynolds, Mildred (Millie)

Norma Jean Pilcher's "mother" had actually been her roommate at the psychiatric hospital. (MOMENTS)

Riata

Fifty thousand acre west Texas ranch belonging to the McGill Family. The ranch was probably in the Lubbock area, considering the presence of Buddy Holly. (TESS)

Rickett, Alexandra

She was every little brother's nightmare: an older and bigger sister who delighted in tormenting her younger sibling. (RUNAWAY)

Rickett, Butchie

Sam leaped into this thirteen-year-old boy on a cross-country vacation just in time to dump a chocolate shake in his lap. To make matters worse, Butchie had a big sister who took delight in tormenting her little brother. Butchie's mother Emma left the family in the original history, and was never seen again. In addition, Butchie never finished high school. Sam helped the boy's father rescue her, and then took out his frustrations on the big sister by suspending her by her ankles over a well until she promised never to torment her brother again. (RUNAWAY)

Rickett, Emma

Now that her children were growing up, she felt disillusioned and unfulfilled and was looking for something to give her life some meaning again. To that end she was reading *The Feminine Mystique*. Her husband Hank felt that she belonged in the home, and scoffed at her plans to go back to school and get her degree. Emma ended up going to college, and they moved to Miami so she could get a doctorate in speech and drama. She's still teaching at a local university.

Rickett, Hank

Here's one of those dads right out of a Jean Shepard story. His idea of a perfect vacation is to stick rigidly to a set schedule. Being the dad makes him boss, he believed, and he scoffed at his wife Emma's abilities and ideas. Hank is what is commonly called a self-made man. After breaking his hip at Florida State, he got a job delivering poultry and eventually owned his own company. For Hank, being a good provider meant giving her and the family everything material they needed. What Emma really needed was for him to provide some emotional support, something he was unwilling or unable to do. The experience of nearly losing his wife must have spurred a change in him, as Emma went to college and began a teaching career, and he retired to play golf and look after the children. (RUNAWAY)

Riker, Commander Dirk

Bingo's commander when he was a Naval Ensign. Riker's wife "initiated" each of the pilots, and Riker didn't think that was "a major problem", because he and she were both (in his word) perverted. He accused Al of the rape and murder of his wife, by virtue of his witnessing the event from a cliff overlooking the beach. Al's buddy Chip Fergeson was driving Al's black Corvette, and took Riker's wife to the beach at her insistence. He tried to come on to her, and when she ran she hit her head on a rock, killing herself. (LISA)

Riker, Marci

Commander Riker's wife. Al was accused of raping and murdering her, but had actually turned her advances down because he was involved with another woman. (LISA)

Riply, Allen

Worked for Florida District Attorney Theodore Moody. He helped Moody push cases through court quickly, even though the accused may have benefited from a more thorough trial. His reputation declined with Moody's after Sam exposed their tactics. (LAST)

'Rock the Redhead'

Hit song by the 1970s rock group King Thunder. Sam had trouble learning it in reheasal but, typically, performed the song well in concert. (ROCK)

Rogers, Dr.

Delivered Billie Jean Crockett's baby. (8½)

Roget

Diane McBride was once married to this man. She never told her new husband Tom about him because she thought that if it wasn't real for Tom, it wouldn't be real for her. Roget was a Frenchman who smuggled arms for the Resistance in the Second World War. He turned his wartime activity into a career, which Diane did not know about. Psychotic and very jealous, Roget kept Diane a virtual prisoner in her own home. Roget calmly told Sam that his (Roget's) psychiatrist told him he was quite mad, then went on to relate the story of how his mother had a Nazi lover and turned in all the Resistance members of his village except for him. The Nazis tortured and killed them all, and Roget killed his mother. He was wanted in New York for murdering his psychiatrist. Sam eventually killed Roget by turning his own knife on him. (HONEY-MOON)

Rose, Maria

The singer who preceded Parker, MacKay and Fields onstage at the Las Vegas Golden Sand. (STAND)

Roselli, Pam

An LAPD uniformed officer who answered the call on Janice DeCaro's murder. Pam has also been seeing Detective Jack Stone/Sam. (DREAMS)

Rosencranz, Burt

Mac Ellroy's neighbor had been nicknamed "Burt the Turtle" by the neighborhood kids. Mac tried to sell him a fallout shelter, but Burt had thought a pool would be a better investment. His wife ran off with the pool man. (NUCLEAR)

Ross, Andrew

Sam found himself playing the final chord of Ross's recital at Carnegie Hall on February 6, 1964. Forced to return for an encore, he played Chopsticks. Ross was blind, having learned to play by ear. Sam, though, could see, and had to learn to do a convincing imitation of a blind man in order to perform his job. (BLIND)

Roundtree, Lyle

Chief of police in the little town of Raven Rock, Massachusetts. He resisted Sam's allegations that the death of Hilla Danner was a murder, and when Sam accused him of being in the pocket of Roger Truesdale, Lyle countered that he was his own man. No one owns him – except maybe his wife. Ziggy says he stays chief for 33 years and then retires to Florida. (DEAR)

Rumplestiltskin

Sam's code word to bring Alia out from under hypnosis. (REVENGE)

Rusty

This World War II vet had a good pitching arm before the war. In fact, several major league teams wanted him. He played AAA ball with Toledo. After four years in the Pacific, though, he tried to resume his career and found his arm was "gone". Rusty harbored a lot of anger and resentment over his situation, and when Machiko MacKenzie came to town he vented his anger in her direction. He painted "Japs Go Home" on their pickup truck, and picked a fight with Sam at the church picnic. When Machiko ran away from the MacKenzie home, Rusty picked her up and took her to his repair shop, presumably with plans to make her pay for his problems. (MACHIKO)

S

St. Cloud, Diana

She ran the Women's Collective, and believed the only way to get men to listen and understand what women had to say was through violence. Her father abused her when she was a child, and she came close to killing him. The FBI had her tied to several subversive groups, but many women followed her blindly, and it was all going to erupt during a protest when she would be shot by the chief of police. When Sam tried to bring a peaceful end to the situation, Diana nearly shot the chief. After spending five years in prison (and burning off a lot of her anger), she became one of the leading activists for changing the constitution. (LIBERATION)

St. Dorothy's Church, Philadelphia

Sam found himself there as a priest in 1963. (FAITH)

St. John, Edward V

Pronounced "Sinjin" in the British manner. When Sam briefly changed Al's history by leaping into him, Al was replaced by St. John, a stiff-upper-lip British gentleman who preferred old-fashioned suits. He called Sam "Samuel", which did not go over well with the time traveler. During this time Sam began to lose his memory of Al in spite of his best efforts. He had no idea who St. John was, and faked being Swiss-cheesed so he could get the new observer's identity. At one point St. John called Bingo a satyr after he started eyeing Tina. After Sam righted history, Al reappeared. (LISA)

St. Mary's Church, Sacramento

Boxer Kid Cody's deceased owner left his contract to the nuns who ran the church. They were praying for Cody to win the championship fight so his winnings would pay for a new chapel and street mission. (HAND)

Sam

Mac and Kate Ellroy's family dog. He was going to survive a nuclear attack in style, right along with his masters, and he had the doggie cape and air mask to prove it. (NUCLEAR)

Sammis, Hank

Ronnie's son. After Sam changed history, Hank went on to win a silver medal in wrestling in the 1968 Olympics. (HEART)

Sammis, Lottie

Terry and Ronnie's mother managed The Battling Rooskies. (CHAMP)

Sammis, Myra

Ronnie's wife was getting tired of the nomadic life the family was leading and wanted to settle down. (CHAMP)

Sammis, Ronnie

One half of the tag-wrestling team called The Battling Rooskies. Ronnie had high hopes of winning a championship and buying his family a house with the winnings, but he was going to die during the big match unless Sam could do something about it. A case of rheumatic fever at the age of eight led to an undiagnosed heart condition, which Sam couldn't get the ring doctor to detect. After Sam won the match, Ronnie checked into a hospital and had his heart condition properly diagnosed and treated. (CHAMP)

Sammis, "Slammin" Sammy

The Sammis brothers' father had worked the wrestling circuit for a decade before he passed away. He never made it to the big time, and his boys were determined to make it. (CHAMP)

Sammis, Terry

Terry had just joined The Battling Rooskies tag-wrestling team the week before Sam leaped into his life. Sam's task was to keep Terry's brother Ronnie from dying during the big upcoming match. (CHAMP)

Sanders, George

He was not pleased when his wife Margaret and daughter Suzie got arrested at a Women's Liberation rally while

Margaret should have been home cooking and serving at a dinner party for two of his employees. He was trying to decide if he should promote Peter Tipton, son of the local police chief and expectant father, or Evy Brownfield, who was just as qualified and had a year of seniority. He felt Peter needed the promotion and raise because he had a child on the way, but he could pay Evy less money because her husband also worked. Besides, it was company policy to pay women less. He threatened to leave Margaret if she didn't stop her activities and be the wife he thought she should be, which meant being there to cook dinners and get the dry cleaning. Sam convinced him that he wouldn't lose his wife just because she wanted to be herself and not what he tried to make her into. George eventually promoted Evy with full pay. (LIBERATION)

Sanders, Margaret

In 1968 this housewife was getting interested in the Women's Liberation movement, and Sam leaped in just in time to burn her bra at a rally. Sam and Margaret's daughter Suzie got arrested, and Sam's picture (as Margaret) made the front page of the paper the next day. As Margaret's husband George tried to put his foot down about his wife and daughter's activities, Sam found himself in the unenviable position of keeping this woman's family together while stopping a second rally from turning to violence. Sam eventually convinced George to try not to mold his wife in the image of "his" Margaret, and the two of them stayed married. Suzie and Margaret went on to stay active in the women's movement and fought for passage of the ERA. (LIBERATION)

Sanders, Suzie

College student and daughter of George and Margaret Sanders. Her father was upset over her participation in the

Women's Liberation movement, and tried to lock her in her room to prevent her from going to a rally. It nearly backfired, and she would have been shot had Sam not abandoned a dinner party to rush to the rally and attempt to talk some sense into both the participants and the law. (LIBERATION)

Sandler, Dr.

Court-appointed physician who evaluated Moe Stein to see if he needed to be committed to an institution. (FUTURE)

Saxton, Ed

Chairman of Saxton Fertilizer and Pesticides of Destiny, New Mexico. (ROBERTO)

Saxton Fertilizer and Pesticides

Large chemical manufacturing plant in Destiny, New Mexico being investigated by Jani Eisenberg of KDNM-TV. They were trying to cover up their secret contract with the Government to develop chemical weapons. Roberto Gutierrez/Sam teamed up with Eisenberg after it became apparent the "UFO people" he was investigating were actually a cleanup crew from Saxton Chemical. Al tagged that the guards at the plant were actually military men by their demeanor. After Sam and Jani discovered the chemical weapons factory hidden with the plant, Ed Saxton conspired to do away with her and pay off Roberto. Sam managed to thwart both plans, and Saxton was arrested. (ROBERTO)

Scooter

A pledge at the Tau Kappa Beta fraternity. He was forced to perform a lot of stunts – many degrading – in order to get initiated. He had to put lobsters in Dean Stomper's mailbox and later steal his basketball autographed by Wilt Chamberlain. He was forced to wear his underwear on the outside of his pants whenever he went to class, and to steal the answers to a chemistry test from the chemistry building. He was the one who died in the original history when the building was bombed. (FRAT)

Scooter was also the name of the Wilson family's cat. (CAM)

Scrubbo, Mr.

While working at a TV station in 1957, Sam found himself dressed up as a giant steel wool pad and singing the joys of "Scrubbo". As Mr. Scrubbo, he was "the housewife's new best friend". (FUTURE)

Scunney, Fr. Mac

The Irish priest at the mostly-Italian St. Dorothy's Church in Philadelphia had become disillusioned and had begun to drink heavily. Mac had a Purple Heart, Silver Star, and several commendations from his days in the 1st Marine Division at Guadalcanal. He survived the Battle of Bloody Ridge, and swore that if he made it through he'd spend the rest of his life making up for it. One of his joys is teaching parish kids how to box. He gave up the bottle, stayed at St. Dorothy's for 20 years, and had two Golden Gloves champs during that time. (FAITH)

Sedlack, Miss

Sam's first grade teacher. Apparently he had a crush on her. (TESS)

Servanovich, Simo

A miner better known by the nickname "Ziggy". See that entry for further details.

Seymour

Ran the news-stand in the building in which Sam (as Nick Allen) worked. Seymour was an orphan, left on a stoop in Greenwich Village. He grew up in the East Side Orphanage and slept in the library because people left him alone there. He was deeply into pulp magazines, and idolized private detective Nick Allen. Sam offhandedly suggested he write hard-boiled detective stories, and launched a new pulp novelist. (SEYMOUR)

Shaefer, Debbie

The producer for Dr. Ruth's radio program had an on-again, off-again relationship with Doug Bridges, the show's announcer. Sam was supposed to get them together, as Dr. Ruth felt they were perfect for each other. After Sam had them talk about their relationship on the air, they broadcast their wedding ceremony. (RUTH)

Shaefer, Vincent A.

He taught at the National Weather Institute, and apparently Billy Beaumont was his star pupil. Schafer actually made it snow in 1946 on the New York-Masachu-setts border using silver iodide. It may have helped that there was a 95% chance of snow anyway. (RAIN)

Sharp, Kenny

A St. Louis actor who was playing, among other roles, Future Boy at a local TV station in 1957. Sam leaped in right in the middle of a broadcast just as they were getting ready to fictionally travel in time. (FUTURE)

Sheldon

A boy at the 4th Street Mission gave Michael Blake this three-legged rocking horse. Santa wasn't coming and it was all he had. (MIRACLE)

Sherman, Lisa, Lt. (US Navy)

A Navy nurse who was Al's girlfriend in 1957. She was killed in the original history in a car accident after Al was placed into custody for a rape and murder he did not commit. She originally told Al's defense counsel that the two of them were at the Sea Breeze Hotel on the night of the murder, which was the truth. She was married, but said her husband slept around on her. As she was driving home, blinded by her tears, she crashed her car and died. The holographic Al showed up too late to prevent that from happening again. To complicate matters, Sam had told Lisa before Al arrived that she shouldn't testify and jeopardize her career. Sam thought he was there to clear Al's name, when instead it was to keep Lisa from dying. With Lisa dead and no alibi, the chances of Al dying in the gas chamber for the crime eventually went up to 100% and he was replaced by St. John. Ziggy attempted a rescue by leaping Bingo into himself the night of the murder in order to follow Chip for the evening, thereby preventing the deaths of both Marci Riker and Lisa Sherman. (LISA)

Shiloh Boys

Weighing in at 538 pounds, this Texas tag-team duo was practically a shoe-in to win the Georgia Wrestle-a-thon. (CHAMP)

Shiloh, Carl

Al described the older and meaner of the Shiloh Boys as "a vending machine with a head on it". Carl had a penchant for tearing doors from their hinges, and Ziggy gave Sam a 75.3% chance that he would kill the time traveler in the title bout. (CHAMP)

Shiloh, Sharon

Carl's wife loved to play a little game of coming on to other men, then watching her husband tear them apart in a jealous rage. Naturally she chose Terry Sammis as a target right after Sam leaped into the wrestler. (CHAMP)

Shiner, Judge

Presided over Abagail Fuller's murder trial. (TRILOGY)

Shriners

Four from Shreveport come to LaBonte's "house", and Sam was so nervous that they might be connected with Gina's disappearance that he finally told them they would have to leave. (COMFORT)

Shump, Lamar

This wrestling promoter was not amused after Sam leaped into Terry Sammis and destroyed his opponent with a well-placed martial arts move. Not only should Terry and his brother have lost, but Lamar had choreographed the match to run much longer than the 1:08 it did. The Battling Rooskies had earned a championship match, but Lamar told them they couldn't win because they were Russians, at least as far as the audience was concerned. (CHAMP)

Shumway

The police investigator handling Katie McBain's rape case. He bet Nancy Hudson his new fishing rod that they could prosecute Kevin Wentworth. (RAPED)

Sigmatron

One of the components of the Accelerator Chamber, it goes on-line seconds before the time traveler leaps. (BACK)

Simon, Dirk

Al's first wife, Beth, married Dirk after she had Al declared dead. (MIA)

Simpson, Ada and Nathaniel

Ada worked for Clyde/Sam. Her son Nathaniel had been hanged by a lynch mob in the original history because he

211

and his friends demonstrated against voter registration in-equity. Nathaniel went on to become one of the first black mayors in Alabama. (JUSTICE)

Skaggs, Sgt. Robert

Detective with the San Diego Police Department, and Sam's partner when he was a cop in 1969. Skaggs had served in Vietnam, and relates that he once froze up in the Delta while on patrol when he came face-to-face with a naked baby standing in the trail. Although he knew it was an ambush, he simply froze. Another soldier knocked him out of the way. He said he figured if a man is lucky, he got to freeze up once in his life and talk about it. Apparently a pair of dope dealers he and Sam arrested overheard that story, because they set up an ambush at a restaurant by placing a baby on a table. Skaggs froze. Sam arrived just in time, blowing them away before they could shoot Skaggs. (MIA)

Skipper, Earl

Station Manager and News Director at KDNM-TV, Destiny, New Mexico. (ROBERTO)

Slater, Steve

Maggie Spontini's fiancé was an attorney who was also acting as her counsel in her divorce. Al cautioned Sam not to trust him. (SPONT)

Smithfield, Dr.

Jimmy LaMotta's doctor at Wayside who felt it would be a good idea for Jimmy to be out in the "real world". (JIMMY)

'Smoke Gets in Your Eyes'

Sam sang this ballad as Davey Parker at the Las Vegas Golden Sand Hotel. (STAND)

Snowball

The lion appearing in the fashion shoot with Edie Landsdale. (STROBE)

Sodium Amytol

Dr. Masters suggested performing experiments on Sam Beederman/Sam using this drug. (SHOCK)

Sodium Pentathol

Widely known as "truth serum", it's also used in some states for executions. Dr. Hardin of Project Blue Book gave a dose to Max Stoddard/Sam and Sam proceeded to reveal many of his personal details, including Project Quantum Leap. (BRIGHT)

'Somewhere in the Night'

Joey DeNardo wrote the music to this song back in 1982 or so before he left Lorraine. Sometime between then and 1985 he put lyrics to the music, and Sam sang it at The Roadside Rendezvous in Tullarosa, NM. (PIANO)

Sonny

A twelve-year-old kid who was baptized by Father Mac of St. Dorothy's in Philadelphia. Father Mac watched him grow up, so it was especially painful when the child was hit by a train and killed. He was murdered because he witnessed a robbery/homicide. (FAITH)

Sophie

She worked at LaBonte's "house" wearing a skimpy Little Bo Peep costume. At LaBonte's birthday party, she presented Gilbert/Sam with her grandfather's glass eye, saying it would bring him good luck. (COMFORT)

A woman named Sophie worked as a guard at Mallard Prison. (REVENGE)

'Southern Salute to America'

Elvis Presley/Sam sang at this Memphis talent show. (MEMPHIS)

Spencer, Admiral

Headmaster at Prescott Naval Academy. (HONOR)

Spencer, Karen

Admiral Spencer's daughter was dating Tommy York. He was a senior, and she a freshman. She was rather concerned because even after three months, Tommy hadn't "you know". (HONOR)

Spokane, Elizabeth

Coed at Meeks College in 1967. Sam, as Knut "Wild Thing" Wileton, was there to keep her from planting a bomb in the chemistry building as a war protest gesture. She was from a rich family, and Al speculated her anti-war stance was part rebellion against her parents, part frustration, and part genuine caring for what was happening in

Vietnam. In the original history she went underground after the bombing. In the end Elizabeth got back together with her parents and became a major player in stopping the war. (FRAT)

Spontini, Harry

Sam leaped into The Great Spontini during the "swords in the basket" routine, just before the Sword of Doom nearly severed his manhood. His dream was to settle down and operate a magic shop. Spontini's wife Maggie had left him and their daughter Jamie in 1971, and has suddenly returned, saying she is going to get married and demanding custody. Al warned Sam that Spontini originally spent everything he had on attorney fees. Sam eventually reunited the family and they did open the magic shop. (SPONT)

Spontini, Jamie

The twelve-year-old daughter of Harry and Maggie Spontini has been working as her dad's assistant and knew as much about the illusions as did Spontini. She's very world-wise, having worked in adult places like nightclubs. After becoming the object of a custody fight between her parents, Jamie ran away and went to the club to work on the Table of Death, an illusion she was working on with Harry. She barely escaped death when Sam rescued her. (SPONT)

Spontini, Maggie

Maggie left her magician husband Harry and their daughter Jamie in 1971, and returned three years later asking for a divorce and custody. During those years, she had obtained her real-estate license and had started a new life. She felt she could give Jamie what she needed, and that she really didn't have a choice when she left the family. Al believed Maggie still loved Harry, and Sam worked to reunite the family. (SPONT)

Spooner, Melvin

The town mortician/coroner of Raven Rock, Massachusetts. Sam leaped into him to solve the murder of Hilla Danner. (DEAR)

Stallone, Sylvester

As a Philadelphia priest in 1963, Sam heard a young boxer at St. Dorothy's lament that he was unable to practice as much because of his new job at a butcher shop. Sam told the kid about a movie he saw once about a fighter who worked at a butcher shop and worked out using the beef hanging in a freezer. "Yo!" the kid said, as he slammed his locker closed, revealing the tag S. STALLONE. (FAITH)

Stand-up comic

Sam has found himself in that occupation twice. The first time was after his simo-leap with Al, when he ended up in the Catskills in 1956. Ziggy said he was there to help a little girl being torn apart by a divorce by getting the comic together with a waitress so they could raise the girl together (BACK). The second time, he was part of a comic trio (STAND).

Stanton, Cherlyn

By 1978 she had been married to Larry Stanton for 28 years, and loved to play bedroom games on Saturday nights. Larry was her second husband. The first one died of a heart attack when she was 17 and he was 77. Al says

Larry Stanton will meet the same fate, and believes she killed both of her husbands. She didn't want her husband to take on defending Abagail Fuller because her black housekeeper Marie showed up to ask him to take the case. She called Marie "nigger trash". Sam apologized for her. (TRILOGY)

Stanton, Lawrence III (Larry)

Small-town Louisiana lawyer. He left town after Abagail Fuller was nearly lynched because he didn't want his children to grow up in an atmosphere of prejudice and hate. He was living in Shreveport in 1978 when Marie Billings came to ask him to defend Abagail Fuller on charges of murdering Leta Aider. Originally he didn't, but Sam was now there and took the case. Stanton had a heart condition, which Sam had "inherited" along with the physical aura, and he had to take nitroglycerine pills to keep going sometimes. (TRILOGY)

Star, blue neon

Apparently the Project symbol in the early days, possibly a holdover from the Star Bright Project. Al wore one in the pilot as did Gooshie, and Al's car sported a large star in the rear window. Al also wore the star during Sam's leap into Dr. Gerald Bryant. (PILOT, CROSSED)

Star Bright Project

Presumably the predecessor to Project Quantum Leap. Sam met Donna just as she was leaving the project, and he and Al met here for the first time. (CROSSED, BALL)

Star Wars

Sam spun the tale to Corey LaMotta as a bedtime story. (JIMMY)

Stathatos, Nikos

When Sam leaped into this Greek sailor the yacht on which he was working had just blown up, and Sam helped rescue Vanessa Foster, heiress and spoiled brat. Born in Piraeus, Greece on February 12, 1935, he didn't seem like a rich girl's type, but Vanessa found herself falling for him, and Sam for her. Nikos had been attracted to her on the yacht, carrying all five of her trunks to her room and putting a mint on her pillow every night. Nikos was an excellent navigator, which was the reason he and Vanessa got picked up so soon in the original history. Sam's lack of said skills got them marooned on a deserted island, and by the time Nikos and Vanessa were picked up nine years later they'd had six children. (SHREW)

Stawpah

One of the people Sam encountered at Al's Place was a man named Stawpah. He was just over 40, but having been crippled with rheumatoid arthritis, no longer worked in the mines. Stawpah distrusted everyone, perhaps because he came from Russia. He insisted to Al the bartender that Sam wasn't who he pretended to be, but once he figured that out, he would know why he (Stawpah) was there. Later, after Tonchi and Pete were trapped in the mine, Stawpah told Sam that he – not Sam – was there for the two men. He also knew the conditions where they were trapped, right down to how far the water had risen.

When questioned about how he could possibly know, Stawpah enigmatically said he had been there before. After the miners were saved, Sam saw Stawpah leap. No one except Sam and the bartender remembered him after that. Gooshie the mailman said that he knew a miner named Stawpah who had died in 1933.

Al had an uncle named Stawpah, presumably his mother's brother. He had also been stricken with rheumatoid arthritis. (MIRROR)

Stein, Moe

A 65-year-old former Shakespearean actor who did very well in the "Scottish Play" (it's bad luck for actors to utter the word "Macbeth"), he found himself playing Captain Galaxy on TV in St. Louis in 1957. Moe honestly believed that time travel was possible and was working on his own machine he called a Timonometer. He had read up on all of the latest theories, and the time machine came close to working. Unfortunately everyone around him thought he was loony, especially his daughter Irene, who tried to have him committed. Is the man crazy, or just eccentric? After the decision to commit had been made, Moe ran off and returned to his home and tried to start his machine. He told Irene he only wanted to go back and change things so he could have spent more time with her and his wife instead of living on the road. Instead of committing him, Irene took him home to live with her, where he spent the rest of his life entertaining the neighborhood kids with tales of the future. (FUTURE)

Steiner, Ben

A Hollywood TV executive who was interested in using Tyler Means' story as the basis for a western series. (GUN)

Stevens, Michelle

A young nursing student in New York who had taken on the job of unpaid assistant to blind concert pianist Andrew Ross. She skipped classes to attend his concerts sometimes, much to the consternation of her mother. She was going to get murdered in Central Park unless Sam could prevent it. (BLIND)

Stevens, Mrs.

Michelle's overbearing mother. Her husband had walked out on the family when Michelle was two, leaving her to fend for the family. She made up for her lack of a life by constantly berating her daughter – telling her she wasn't pretty, that she wasn't good enough for the likes of Andrew Ross. She finally decided to let go of Michelle and at last have a life of her own. (BLIND)

Stilbart, Phillip

Initially Sam and Al suspected this oddly-behaving fan of plotting to kill Tonic, the lead singer for King Thunder. He had been stalking the rock star for some time with a camera, dogging him at personal appearances. Born July 27, 1957 to Priscilla Stilbart, the identity of his father was unknown. She raised him, and died in 1970, two years after they lost their farm. Sam finally confronted him and learned that Phillip believed Tonic to be his father. The band had played in Omaha the first time they came over from England, and Phillip showed Sam a picture of Tonic and Priscilla supposedly taken after the concert. After showing Sam that he has the same web of skin between his fingers as Tonic, Ziggy then gave a 98% chance that Tonic was Phillip's dad. The band offered him a job as a roadie, and eventually he became one of the hottest studio musicians in London. (ROCK)

Stoddard, John

Max Stoddard's son. He didn't believe in his father's tales of UFOs, and decided the best thing to do was to commit him to a mental hospital. (BRIGHT)

Stoddard, Maxwell

This 79-year-old man hadn't talked about anything but spaceships and flying saucers for two months before Sam leaped in on May 21, 1966. Sam saw a UFO flying overhead, but no one believed him when he reported it. That was the trouble with Stoddard, too. His son eventually had him committed to a mental institution.

Stoddard kept a scrapbook of UFO-related articles and records for fifty years, and had found the town had a history of UFO sightings. There had been two in 1962, one in June of 1958, and two in January of 1955 – one of those on New Year's Day. Ziggy found that there was a new sighting approximately every 47.51 months, and then a second sighting 3-4 days after the first.

But Sam had more on his mind that proving UFOs exist and keeping Stoddard out of the mental institution. His grandson Tim was seventeen and wanted to be a musician, but kept butting heads with Max's son John. If Sam didn't do something to help Tim, he was going to run away and die of a heroin overdose.

After Tim and John realized the men from Project Blue Book had effectively kidnapped Stoddard/Sam, they helped him escape. To everyone's amazement, the UFO returned as predicted, and Sam leaped as Max came back in time to take the ride of his lifetime. (BRIGHT)

Stoddard, Tim

Max Stoddard's 17-year-old grandson wanted to be a musician, but he didn't see eye-to-eye with his dad who wanted him to either go to college or get a job. He decided to run away to New York, where Ziggy said he would play a couple of performances with a small-time band called River Wind, then end up on a slab at Bellevue dead of a heroin overdose. Tim helped his father take Sam to the mental hospital, but noticed the government car in the parking lot, and in an amazing act of cooperation for a father and son who didn't get along, helped rescue Max/Sam at gunpoint. (BRIGHT)

Stoltz, Miss

Her name might as well have been Frau Blucher; this creepy housekeeper for Troian Claridge certainly fit the part. Troian had hired her after Julian had died to look after the house. She was the only one who applied to an ad in the *Lakeview Weekly*, claiming she used to work there as a girl. Troian guessed she was Pennsylvania Dutch, possibly Mennonite, from her strange ways and word usage such as "redding up" the kitchen. After an earthquake, it was revealed that Nathaniel Claridge's wife was a Stoltz, a Mennonite from Pensylvania. The earthquake had brought up Priscilla's body from the lake, and when Sam and Troian lifted the sheet, they saw a woman who looked exactly like Miss Stoltz. At that moment, the housekeeper vanished. (TROIAN)

Stone, Chad

A real hunk of a stunt man working on *Disco Inferno* and *Earthquake*. Sam was there to see that Chad's brother Chris did not die attempting a stunt. (DISCO)

Stone, Chris

Brother of Chad, he was training to be a stunt man like his brother and father. Chris never got along very well his his father, probably because his mother raised him. Chris was desperate to please his father by getting his stunt man's card, but deep down really wanted to be a singer. After he nearly died attempting a stunt, Sam convinced his father that Chris should pursue his own choices in life. (DISCO)

Stone, Lt. Jack

Sam leaped into this LAPD detective just as he discovered the horribly mutilated body of Janice DeCaro. Something happened during the leap, and a small piece of Stone got left behind in Sam. This part was a dream/flashback that was apparently triggered when Stone saw the body. These dreams became more intense, and Sam saw *his* own death, which was nearly facilitated by Dr. Mason Crane. (DREAMS)

Stormer, Samantha

"I'm going to be called by my own name," Sam sighed as he sank into the bubble bath. What he found out seconds later was that Sam was short for Samantha, and he was going to be the youngest executive secretary at National Motors Corporation. Samantha's boss was a silver-tongued devil named Buddy Wright, who felt that the lovely secretary was just another perk of the job. The married Wright was also dating Samantha's roommate Gloria Collins, who would later try to kill herself after she found Buddy was not going to marry her. (GLORIA)

When her personality "filled in" for Sam's at Havenwell, Samantha smoked a cigarette and believed she was there because she hit Buddy Wright. She also said she knew a Sam Beckett in Elk Ridge, Illinois, but that he was just a boy she knew a long time ago. (SHOCK)

Stratton, Peg

Tom Stratton's wife. Pregnant with their second child, she went into early labor when Tom/Sam crashed the X-2 experimental aircraft. Sam's Swiss-cheese brain remembered he was in med school and suggested a 5% alcohol solution be fed intravenously. It made her instantly drunk, but also stopped the contractions. The baby was born full-term and named Samantha. (PILOT)

Stratton, Tom, Capt. (USAF)

When Sam leaped for the first time, he found himself in the life of this Air Force test pilot. Ziggy postulated his job was to break Mach 3 in the X-2 and live. The only problem was that Sam knew nothing about flying an aircraft. Al helped him fly, but couldn't help him land, so Sam bailed out after he hit Mach 3. And still hadn't leaped. After he stopped Peg's premature labor, he leaped as his son Mikey was tossing him a baseball. (PILOT)

Briefly, his personality surfaced when Sam was in Havenwell. The first thing he asked Al was if he broke Mach 3 in the X-2. (SHOCK)

String Theory

Sam's string theory of time was developed with Professor Sebastian LoNigro of MIT in the summer of 1973, and forms the basis for Project Quantum Leap. When Sam first leaped, the theory was Swiss cheesed out of his brain. Al had just given a "Dick and Jane" explanation to Congress and the President, and gave it to Sam:

> Al: One end of this string represents your birth. The other end, your death, You tie the ends together, and your life is a loop. Ball the loop, and the days of your life touch each other out of sequence. Therefore, leaping from one point of the string to another . . .
>
> Sam: Would move you backward or forward within your own lifetime.
>
> Al: Which is our project – Quantum Leap! (PILOT)

In 1957, Moe Stein had almost worked out the string theory, but his version had the traveler going very fast along the loop. Sam balled the string up and showed Moe the rest of the theory. (FUTURE)

After nearly five years of leaping, Sam discovered that he could also leap along his own DNA. This happened when he leaped into John Beckett, his great-grandfather who was serving in the Union Army during the Civil War. (STATES)

Styles, Leon

At 26, the illiterate drifter had committed a string of serial murders, and had just escaped custody after killing two deputies and seriously wounding a third when Sam leaped in. Styles was holed up in a house holding a woman and her daughter hostage, and Sam had to make sure the sheriff didn't kill Styles in retaliation for his daughter's death. Back in the Waiting Room, Styles had overpowered a Marine guard, taken his gun, and left the Project in Gooshie's car. Styles was eventually returned to the Waiting Room and Sam leaped. (KILLIN)

Sun Ray Airlines

Marty Ellroy flew into Florida on this carrier. (TALE)

Sun Records

Elvis Presley cut his first record at their Memphis studios, as a birthday gift for his mom. (MEMPHIS)

Super Bowl XXX

Al was watching this game while Sam, as Eddie Vega, was quarterbacking the Jaguars against the Bulldogs for the city championship. Al said the Steelers were down by three. (ALL)

Svensen, Jack

Arnold Watkins' roommate was pledging Chi Kappa Delta. It was no use to talk him out of it, because his great-grandfather was one of the founders of the fraternity. (RETURN)

Swiss-Cheese Effect

During the initial leap, Sam didn't know anything about himself except "It worked. What worked?" and a telephone number. Al described Sam's brain as being "magnafoozled" by the leap (PILOT). While he has regained many pieces of his memory, any bit is likely to leave again when he leaps, leaving his memory with holes, hence the Swiss cheese metaphor. When Sam returned to PQL, the holes in his memory plugged and he began to lose memory of his previous leaps (BACK). Using Swiss cheese as a model, the large holes can represent things like the Leaper's mother and father, and the small holes are simple things (REVENGE).

Sybil

Fortune teller at the circus where Sam worked as Victor Panzini. She sensed Al's presence in the room, but did not see him. She also correctly predicted that Eva would fall the next night if her father were to attempt to catch her, but she couldn't say how she knew. It just came to her. When she looked into Sam's eyes, she said that he had been reincarnated many times, as she could see a lot of souls. (NET)

T

TKO

One amazingly strong drink with a little bit of everything thrown in, including dry ice to make smoke and an ice cube that has been passed hand-to-hand down the bar. This was Kid Cody's favorite "training" drink. (HAND)

Table of Death

An escape trick Harry Spontini and his daughter Jamie were working on. They had an audition with Bill Bixby, and if the illusion worked well, it would be used on his series *The Magician* and they would have been paid $3,500. The escape routine involved a table, to which the magician was shackled; above was a canopy consisting of 900 pounds of knives, which would come down if the shackles weren't opened in fifteen seconds – a real test of the magician's lock-picking ability. The table got its name because two people had already died on it. (SPONT)

Taggert, Sheriff

Pursued Sam and George Wakashie to the reservation after they broke out of the jail where they were being held for stealing a pickup truck. (FREEDOM)

Takins, Pervis

Abagail Fuller had been baby-sitting this seven-year-old when she told him she was going to get married. He had a crush on Abagail, and ran off because he didn't want her to get married. The townspeople thought Abagail had something to do with his disappearance, and tried to lynch her. Sam had Al find the child's whereabouts, which saved Abagail. (TRILOGY)

Tales of Gore

A comic book Corey LaMotta often read to his uncle Jimmy. (JIMMY)

Tallawaga County Prison

Work Prison 1 was located so far out in the woods that the state had no idea how badly it was run. They would make up the rules as they went along, tacking extra time on to sentences when prisoners committed minor infractions. It was shut down three months after Sam and Jasper Boone escaped. (UNCHAINED)

Tanner, Chuck

Pseudonym of Joey DeNardo. (PIANO)

Tamino, Blue

A worker at the Oakland Docks who constantly taunted Jimmy LaMotta because he was retarded. He set Jimmy up for a number of blunders. Sam discovered Blue was dyslexic and had been covering it up. (JIMMY)

Tate, Elizabeth (Liz)

After her husband beat her for the fifteenth time, she shot him, which landed her in Mallard Prison for a life sentence. In the original history, Liz was wrongly executed for the murder of fellow inmate Carol Benning. Sam leaped into Liz and Alia had leaped into her companion Angel Jenson, which meant Sam had to save all three women. Sam was able to prove that the warden was indirectly responsible for Benning's death. (REVENGE)

Taylor, Dawn

As the homecoming queen and girlfriend of Chi Kappa Delta president Mike Hammond, she might have been able to convince Arnold Watkins to give up his Midnight Marauder routine. Alia was leaped into her for precisely this reason, and tried to goad Arnold/Sam into a confrontation with Hammond until she realized who Arnold actually was. (RETURN)

Taylor, Willis

Billie Jean Crockett and her boyfriend Willis promised they'd never see each other again after she got pregnant, and she arranged to give the baby up for adoption. After Sam leaped into the teenager to help her keep the baby, he went to see Willis about the possibility of his helping support the child. But he didn't want to jeopardize his job or his college scholarship, and refused. (8½)

Taylor's Diner

Sue Anne and Julie Winters worked at this Memphis eatery, and this is where Elvis Presley/Sam finally convinced Mr. Phillips to give him an audition. (MEMPHIS)

Telipha

A star in Ursa Major "born" in 1956, the year Sam was a standup comic in the Catskills. (BACK)

Thames

Zoey's observer enjoyed every minute of his stint as a hologram – except the last. He was a fan of James Brown and always carried a walking stick. Pronounced "Tems" like the river in Great Britain. (REVENGE)

Thatcher, Margaret

The future Prime Minister of Britain was aboard the Queen Mary during Sam's short cruise. (BRIDE)

Thailer, Mrs. Cassy

She brought the adoptions papers by for Billie Jean Crockett to sign, and was dismayed to find that she had changed her mind about giving up the baby. (8½)

Thomas, Shane "Funnybone"

Shane had been riding with the Cobras motorcycle gang for about a week when Sam leaped into him. "Bone", as he was affectionately known, was the sort of clown of the gang. He drew caricatures of others and rode a 1957 Harley Sportster, which Al pointed out had a 55 cc. motor with overhead valves. Sam leaped into Bone to save the life of Becky – a girl who was riding with the gang and infatuated with Dillon, their leader. (REBEL)

Through and through

A police term describing a bullet that passes completely through the body. (LAST)

Thurlow, Joe

In a May-December romance, twenty-five-year-old Joe was living with fifty-year-old Jane Lindhurst in 1969. While her son saw the actor as a gigolo, Joe honestly loved her and wanted to get married. While performing Hamlet in the nude, Joe/Sam was spotted by an ad agency to be the next Boxer Boy in the underwear ads. This was the break Joe needed. (PLAY)

Timonometer

Moe Stein's time machine. The first time he fired it up it blew up pretty spectacularly, but he said it was just a few minor parts. After he repaired the machine the next day, Moe fired it up again, and there was a bit of a leaping effect trying to start, but the machine failed to work. (FUTURE)

Time Patrol

1957 children's television program featuring Captain Galaxy and Future Boy, and their adventures in time and space. Apparently the program was syndicated, as mail came from as far away as Wyoming. It was produced in St. Louis. (FUTURE)

Tina

Al's most-time girlfriend/lover. The woman Al picked up in the pilot was identified as Tina, but she's obviously not the same Tina, as Al and his Tina met in Las Vegas over a poker game. Al had a flush. She had a pair (TESS). Sam never remembered her until he briefly leaped back to the Project (BACK). Her name, according to Al, is in a tattoo "on a super-secret part of her anatomy". Al also claimed Tina thought Sam was kind of cute (TESS).

When Sam leaped back to 1999, Tina appeared to be very ditzy. Ziggy told Sam during this time that she was having an affair with Gooshie (BACK). In the alternate history, Pulse Communications Technician Tina is married to Gooshie (LISA). When Tina had an affair with the programmer, Al was crushed, saying "She took my second most favorite organ and stomped it to death with her four-inch spike heels." Tina later told Al that she only saw Gooshie to make Al jealous, then gave the programmer a case of mouthwash and sent him packing (TESS).

Al used Tina in every sense of the word. At one point he had her sleep with Weitzman and he blackmailed the Committee head with the information in order to regain his job (CROSSED). Tina owns either a crocodile or an alligator that she keeps in a pit (TESS, TROIAN). By the Dr. Ruth leap, Al and Tina had been going out for a little over four years (RUTH).

Tipton, Don

Chief of police in the town where the Sanders family lived. Perhaps he was trying to help out his son's chances for promotion at George Sanders' firm, for when Margaret and Suzie got arrested he let them go, and also fixed it so their names wouldn't be turned over to the FBI as possible radicals. (LIBERATION)

Tipton, Dora

Pregnant wife of Peter, who in public acted like the dumb, obedient wife. (LIBERATION)

Tipton, Peter

One of two people George Sanders was considering for promotion. He was all for supporting the "traditional" family, which meant women shouldn't be in the work force. He also helped perpetuate stereotypes by trying to think for his pregnant wife. His father was the chief of police. (LIBERATION)

Togo

Shoshone for grandson. (FREEDOM)

Tonic

Lead singer in the 1970s rock band King Thunder. His real name is Geoffrey Mole, but he got the nickname Tonic from a drinking escapade after a concert in Omaha, when he drank too many vodka tonics and had to be taken to a hospital. (ROCK)

Tony

Samantha Stormer dated this married man in 1959. He wouldn't leave his wife for her. (GLORIA)

Torelli, Fr. Vincent

Murdered by Jesus Ortega on September 9, 1969. On his deathbed, he identified Ortega and Raul Casta as his assailants. (LAST)

Trafford, Melanony Elizabeth Charlotte

"Miz Melny" was the widow of Charles Trafford, former governor of Alabama. While she was aware of the racial injustices in the country, she didn't feel it was her place to do anything about it. After she helped Jesse Tyler's granddaughter gain admission to the emergency room of a whites-only hospital, she realized maybe it *was* her place to do something about the injustice. (COLOR)

Travis, Janine

A nineteen-year-old girl who worked as a stripper in a local club was thought to be the latest victim of a Chinatown killer, but the murder turned out to be a copycat case. (EYES)

Truesdale, Greg

His father ran the Truesdale Lodge in Raven Rock, Massachusetts. Greg dated Hilla Danner, and got her pregnant. That interfered with his father's plans to send his son to college and then take over the family business, so his father was quite pleased that Hilla had killed herself. Ziggy says that Greg went to Harvard law school and became a divorce lawyer, but never married. (DEAR)

Truesdale, Roger

Owner of Truesdale Lodge in Raven Rock, MA. He's a very powerful man, and apparently got Melvin Spooner the job of coroner. He fired his employee Hilla Danner over her relationship with Greg, probably in an attempt to get Greg to forget about her. When he found that Hilla was pregnant with Greg's baby, he tried to arrange for an abortion, but Hilla couldn't go through with it. (DEAR)

Trump, Donald

Sam ferried a young boy and his father to a broker's meeting in New York. When Sam mentioned he knew that real estate was going to boom, the boy's face lit up. Sam then pointed down the street and said that someday there might be a big glass tower next to Tiffany's. (WONDERFUL)

Tucker, Dr. Max

Head of animal research for Project Mercury. (WRONG)

Turnsdale Road

The Beckett farm is located ten miles from the freeway along this road. (LAND)

Twilly, Bunny

Daughter of Mustang's owner Margret Twilly. She's had a thing for most men, it seems, but Chuckie Myerwich and Doc Fuller seemed to be high on the list. In fact, in the original history Chuckie was kicked off the team after the two of them were caught together. Sam attempted to rescue the drunken Chuckie, but instead he was caught by Margret and both of them were tossed from the team. (BALL)

Twilly, Margret

Owner of the Galveston Mustangs baseball team. Doc Fuller probably kept his spot on the team because he let her "evaluate his performance" often. (BALL)

Tyler, Ernie

Ran a roadhouse about an hour out of Big Sur. His son Darrell was a Marine who won the Navy Cross and fought off the enemy single-handed at the Chosin Reservoir. In 1958 he was still M.I.A., and a few years later Ernie would find out he was killed in action. In the meantime, he was keeping his son's Christmas and birthday presents, and his motorcycle – a 1949 Black Shadow. In the original history, Ernie died a few months after he found out about his son's death. But after a girl named Becky, who was hanging out with the Cobras, decided to stay, history was changed, as he was still alive in the late 1990s. (REBEL)

Tyler, Jesse

The first person of color into whom Sam leaped. At first, Sam didn't realize he was in Alabama in 1955 when he sat down at the lunch counter of a diner. That incident began a string of troubles which led to a cross-burning and Jesse's granddaughter Nell being nearly killed when a couple of men ran her car off of the road. (COLOR)

When Sam was at Havenwell and Jesse's personality took over briefly, he told the doctors he sat down at the lunch counter because he was hungry and didn't belong in a loony bin because of it. He was 70 years old in 1955, had rheumatism and couldn't read. Upon being shown an ink blot, Sam/Jesse identified it as a mess of burnt chitlins. A second ink blot reminded him of Nell's blood after her accident, and he remembered that at the time he knew the proper medical procedure. His family were sharecroppers, and his parents had been slaves. The third inkblot he identified as the subatomic structure of a quark, asking, "What the hell is a quark?" (SHOCK)

Tyler, Ross

Dylan Powell's cameraman and newsgathering partner was about to get laid off along with Powell, so he concocted a scheme to save their jobs – a string of serial killings in Chinatown. A former Army electronics expert, he rigged up a device to call Powell with a taped message while they were both at the station, thereby diverting suspicion from him. It worked, until psychic Tamlyn Matsuda discovered he was the killer. (EYES)

U

U-2

Not the rock group, as Sam's Swiss-cheese brain thought, but a spy plane piloted by Gary Powers that was shot down. It was a major issue during the Cold War, and Al tried to get Sam to abort the mission in an attempt to prove to Congress that he was indeed back in time (HONEYMOON). A U-2 code-named "Race Car" was being flown out of Japan over the Soviet Union (LHO).

UFO

When Sam leaped into Max Stoddard, he spotted an Un-identified Flying Object which he described as a self-illuminated elliptical orb roughly 15 meters on the long axis, 20 on the short, hovering approximately 20 meters above the ground with no apparent means of pro-pulsion. (BRIGHT)

Unabelle's Bait & Rest

During hurricane Camille, this inland establishment was used as a shelter. (HURRICANE)

United Federal

A conglomerate which wanted to buy Henderson's Bakery
from Michael Blake. (MIRACLE)

V

Van Berg, Elsa & Lisel

A pair of gorgeous twins who were customers at Bianca's beauty salon. Al drooled while Sam fussed over them and promised to do something "nasty" to their hair. (PERM)

Vega, Eddie

Sam leaped into this high school football quarterback just in time to execute a bumbling play that turned into a touchdown for the Jaguars. Sam was there to see that Eddie's best friend Chuey Martinez didn't throw next week's big championship game. (ALL)

Vega, Manuel

Eddie Vega's father owned a mobile restaurant he called Taco Vega. His wife had died in childbirth when Eddie's sister Maria was born, and he never remarried. Manuel's life's ambition was to scrape enough money together to own a restaurant, and he was very close to purchasing one. His neighbor Celia Martinez suggested he buy more catering trucks. He was very fond of the woman, and it's obvious she was taken with him, but they never got beyond the "neighborly" stage. When Sam suggested they marry, the pair had very little trouble agreeing that was an excellent idea. Taco Vega eventually became a million-dollar catering business. And along with the money, they made Jessie, Donna Linda, Carmelina and Rosa. (ALL)

Venus

The goddess of love, born from the sea. Also the second planet in our solar system. Sam pointed it out in the night sky to Vanessa Foster. (SHREW)

Vermullen, Mary Jo

Barbara Whitmore's real name. (NORMA)

Vernon, Gus

The president of the bank in Elk Ridge had been lending money to a lot of farmers who were really unable to pay it back. The reason was he was in on a deal with a developer and was making a fortune in kickbacks from procuring the lands so the developer could build a mall. Gus was a couple of years ahead of Tom in high school, and ran for class president, but was disqualified when he was found stuffing the ballot boxes. Vernon was eventually convicted of bank fraud, served six months, and had his license revoked. (LAND)

Vivian

All she really wanted was to be the good guy, and this guard at Mallard Correctional Facility for Women got her chance when she helped Sam and Alia escape. After Sam told her who he really was, she shook her head and hoped it was a drug flashback from the '60s. Vivian eventually became the warden at Mallard. (REVENGE)

Vlad

Nigel Corrington's dog was undoubtedly named for Vlad the Impaler, the Transylvanian prince who provided the factual basis for the legend of Count Dracula. The dog was killed by a wound to the neck, presumably the work of Victor Drake. (BLOOD)

'Volare'

Al taught Sam the song after he was asked to perform it at an Italian wedding. Sam is obviously a quick student, as he picked the Italian words up as Al carelessly tossed them off to him while occupied with the low cut of a woman's dress. Volare means "fly away" in Italian (DOUBLE). Al also used to sing this song in his sleep, causing one of his wives to charge him with mental cruelty (RAPED).

W

WAPL

Sam created this upstate New York radio station to cover up his futuristic remark to Rachel Porter. While working on the station console, soldering iron in hand, he remarked that it was just like at Apple. It's a reference to the early days at Apple Computer, started by two guys in a garage. (PEORIA)

WCI, Chicago

Their mobile unit arrived to cover the story at WOF in Peoria. (PEORIA)

WFGF, Detroit

Broadcast live King Thunder's appearance at a local mall. (ROCK)

WOF 730 AM

The Peoria radio station that caused a stir for playing rock and roll music. (PEORIA)

Waco Bombers

Minor league baseball team on which Tim Fox finished his career. Sam leaped in to Fox for just long enough to win the player's final game. (PILOT)

Wahorsky

The man at the switch at the state prison in Florida. (LAST)

Waiting Room

Here is where they hold the person who has switched places with Sam. At the Project they see that person as Sam. Once Sam described the room as being all-white, but later it was shown as being chroma key blue. People in the Waiting Room are called visitors. (ROBERTO, LISA)

People in the Waiting Room are just as confused and Swiss-cheesed as Sam, which leads to trouble sometimes. When Leonard Dancey was there, he sat in a fetal position and screamed, "Take me to your leader, I'm a lawyer!" (HELP)

Jesus Ortega was being strapped into the electric chair when Sam leaped in, so he believed that he was already dead and slipped into a sort of comatose state, unable to answer any questions. (LAST)

Maxwell Stoddard was convinced he was on his way to Venus. He kept saying "Take me to your leader," so Al turned him over to Gooshie, saying the programmer was the king of the planet Halitosis. (BRIGHT)

Larry Stanton thought he was dead and that Al was St. Peter and he was going to send the lawyer to Hell for over-charging his hours. (TRILOGY)

Billie Jean Crockett thought she was having her baby in an alien spaceship. (8½)

Rape victim Katie McBain arrived all rolled up in the fetal position and could do nothing but shake for a while. (RAPED)

Dr. Ruth Westheimer did just fine. In fact, Ziggy postulated she was there to help Al. (RUTH)

If the visitor is outside of the Project, and probably specifically the Waiting Room, Sam cannot leap. (KILLIN)

Walker, Gen. Edwin

An attempt was made on his life on April 10, 1963, and Sam leaped into Lee Harvey Oswald just as he was running from the scene. (LHO)

Walters, Charlie "Black Magic"

The greatest pool player in Chicago was a living legend in 1954, but his eyesight was about gone. Two years earlier, he had beat Teddy Fantastic at the Palace at Pittsburgh by running 240 balls in a row. Walters also beat Mosconi in Detroit. He lived out his semi-retirement with his granddaughter Violet at the pool hall she bought and converted into a blues club. The only problem was that she had to get a loan from a shark to do the conversion, and the marker was bought by Eddie Davis, a sleazeball whom Magic normally wouldn't play. Sam had two days to learn to shoot pool so he could win the marker back from Eddie. (POOL)

Walters, John

The youngest of three brothers who held up the bank in Elk Ridge, he was still in school in 1971 when the hold-up took place. He was later convicted of illegal entry, but the judge gave him probation. (LAND)

Walters, Lynelle

One-third of a singing group called The Dovettes. She's destined to run away from home on April 9, 1963 unless Sam can prevent it. If she did run away, she would end up in a slave contract with a sleazy promoter named Bobby Lee. (SONG)

Walters, Mary

She supported her boys in their bid to rob the bank of the money they needed to pay off their loan, and accused the bank manager of murdering their way of life. (LAND)

Walters, Neil

One of three brothers who robbed the bank in Elk Ridge. He had enlisted in the Marine Corps in 1979, and took a compassionate discharge after his father died a year later so he could come home and run the farm. Al described him as a loose-cannon. He was angry because he had to come back and run the farm while his brother William stayed in college, and angry that William wasn't there when he was needed. He was also upset that he couldn't be more like William, who was dad's favorite. But Sam told him that he did the right thing by being there when his dad needed him, and that by being there when his dad died he had a moment that his brother never had, and no one could take that from him. After Sam found the needed evidence to stave off foreclosure, Neil was convicted of aggravated assault and served five years in prison. After he got out, he drifted around the country doing odd jobs and got killed during a robbery in New Orleans in 1977. (LAND)

Walters, Rev.

Chicago Baptist minister and widower father of Lynelle. His wife, Sylvia, died of unknown causes in 1958. Lynelle hated her father because he was stern, and believed her mother had died because she hated her husband, but Sylvia was dying anyway, and had tried to leave the family when she discovered her prognosis. In the original history, Lynelle ran away and they never spoke again. He died after the church burned down in 1972. Sam brought the two together, and it could be inferred her presence helped keep him going after the fire. (SONG)

Walters, Violet

Charlie "Black Magic" Walters' granddaughter owned a blues club and let her Poppy have a pool table in the back. She was a shrewd businessperson, and the club was making a profit. Unfortunately the only way she could raise the capital to start the club was to go to a loan shark, as banks weren't too keen on lending money to black people in 1954. (POOL)

Walters, William, Jr.

An Elk Ridge man whose life paralleled Sam's in several ways. He went on to be an honor student at Indiana State University, but was not home when his dad died, and was unable to come home in time to help save the family farm from foreclosure. When Sam leaped into William, he and his brothers were robbing the bank in Elk Ridge to get enough money to pay back their bank loan. Twisted logic, but the brothers were desperate. After getting some information from Ziggy, Sam deduced that the bank manager Gus Vernon was in on a scheme to sell the foreclosed land to developers. William was later convicted of illegal entry, but the judge gave him probation. (LAND)

Ward, Det. Arnie

A true Beverly Hills Cop investigating the shooting at Phil's Pharmacy. It turned out he was the one who had murdered Phil Hartman, paid to do it by a lady named Chloe, who was dealing drugs. (PERM)

Washakie, George

Sam leaped into this 25-year-old Shoshone Indian as he was being beaten by the local sheriff. George had just broken his grandfather Joseph out of a nursing home, stolen a pickup truck and was on his way back to the reservation with Joseph. Sam's task is to get the old man back to where he was born, because that's where he wanted to die. (FREEDOM)

Washakie, Joseph

This 72-year-old full-blooded Shoshone Indian was dying of emphysema and wanted to expire in his homeland. While he knew of many of the old ways and adhered to them, he was not above using the new ways. He showed Sam an "old Indian trick" for making fire. After chanting and sprinkling sand around the wood, he reached into his pocket and produced a lighter. He also loved to listen to the Redskins – "the best damn team in America" – and was delighted when they beat the Cowboys. Joseph died as Sam carried him across the river to the reservation. (FREEDOM)

Washakie, Suzanne

Older sister of George Washakie. She was a school teacher, and had placed her grandfather Joseph in a state-run nursing home because of his emphysema. (FREEDOM)

Washarski, Frankie

A waitress who was trying to join the comedy team of Parker and MacKay. MacKay didn't want her around because he was afraid to admit he was crazy about her. In the end, the two got married and formed their own comedy team. (STAND)

Washinksi, Max

Michael Blake's childhood friend still lived in the old neighborhood in 1962, selling chestnuts. (MIRACLE)

Watergate Hotel

Donna Elesee's father, Col. Wojohowitz, stayed there, and Sam took her down to see him on June 17, 1972, the same night as the infamous break-in. (CROSSED)

Waters, Denton

Leta Aider tried to retain this high-powered attorney to prosecute Abagail Fuller in the death of her daughter. Denton explained that he couldn't take the case because Abagail was a juvenile at the time of the murder, so she couldn't be tried as an adult. Leta was then found on the floor of Abagail's kitchen with her throat slashed, and

Denton was the prosecuting attorney in Abagail's trial on charges of murdering Leta Aider. (TRILOGY)

Watkins, Arnold

Sam leaped into Arnold as, in the guise of the Midnight Marauder, he was trying to break up a fraternity hazing by hanging on to the front of a car during a chicken race. Arnold seemed to be charmed. He had always escaped death, even when he pulled a coed out of the path of a speeding car. Actually, Arnold was just lucky. He had a death wish after seeing his parents die in a shooting when he was seven. (RETURN)

Watts Riots

This historical event was just beginning on August 11, 1965, as Sam leaped into Watts medical student Ray Harper. There was nothing Sam could do to stop the violence, it had already begun. (B&W)

Wayne

A hand on the Riatta ranch. Ziggy said Tess McGill would marry someone who gave her love letters. After Sam finally found himself falling in love with her, Wayne appeared with a stack of letters he had written her but had never sent. She read them and fell in love with Wayne. (TESS)

Wayside

The institution in which Jimmy LaMotta stayed before coming to live with his brother's family. (JIMMY)

Weitzman

The head of the Committee overseeing PQL favored stovepipe hats. AT one point he was at the Foundation trying to pull the plug on the project. When Al gave Sam some personal information (a big taboo), Weitzman had the observer fired. Al set Weitzman up with Tina and blackmailed him to get his job back. (CROSSED)

Wentworth, Kevin

He raped Katie McBain on June 20, 1980, but was found not guilty at his trial. When he went to talk to Katie after the trial, Sam was still Katie and when Kevin tried a second time, Sam/Katie beat him up. (RAPED)

West, Red

Elvis Presley's best friend always seemed to be getting the future King of Rock and Roll out of scrapes. (MEMPHIS)

Westheimer, Dr. Ruth

Sam leaped into this famous sex therapist in the middle of her call-in radio program as a listener was asking if the size of a man's feet was related to the size of his love muscle. While Sam was there (according to Ziggy) to get her announcer and producer together, Sam found himself fighting for Annie Wilkins, a victim of sexual harassment. The prudish Dr. Beckett had trouble fielding many questions asked of the doctor, but in the process of warning one caller against using silicon breast implants, he convinced 421 women not to have them. These women would have suffered adverse effects in the future. Sam saved Annie's life (after a spectacular dash over car roofs in midtown Manhattan) and got the two lovebirds together. So why hasn't he leaped? The real Dr. Ruth has been counseling Al in the future, and once she got him on to admit he loved Tina, Sam and Dr. Ruth leaped. (RUTH)

'Whatever Will be Will Be (Que Sera Sera)'

This Doris Day song was playing on the radio when Sam leaped into Tom Stratton. Later Peg sang it when she was drunk on the alcohol (5% solution) they used at Sam's suggestion to stop her contractions. (PILOT)

White, Clifford

After Tom Jarret was presumed dead in World War II, Clifford proposed to Suzanne Elsinga, Jarret's finacée. He never served in the war, having been declared 4-F, but there was suspicion he faked his condition to the Draft Board. Sam knocked him off Lovers' Leap just as he was about to do in Tom/Al and Suzanne. (BACK)

Whitmore, Barbara

She got herself a position as Marilyn Monroe's assistant. At one point Barbara told Sam that she was from Tyrone, Ohio and her husband had died in the service. Actually, her name was Mary Jo Vermullen, and she was born in Pasadena, California and had belonged to the Actors' Guild since she was twelve years old. She was using her position and Marilyn Monroe's fragile condition to try and get her own shot at stardom. (NORMA)

Whittler

Head of security for the band King Thudner. (ROCK)

Wickless, Dr.

Head doctor at Havenwell Hospital. (SHOCK)

Widowmaker

Tess McGill was the only one who could ride that wild horse until Sam did as the last test to win her hand. (TESS)

Wild Willie's Western World

A Colorado tourist trap that was the home of giant vegetables, two-headed snakes and Buffalo Chimps. (RUNAWAY)

Wiles, Jake

While Jasper Boone was rotting in prison for a robbery he didn't commit, Jake Wiles continued the robbery spree, in black face. He was put up to it by Cooley, a guard at the Tallawaga Country Prison. Jake began to have second thoughts about the arrangement after Sam identified him as the robber, and the next morning he was found dead. (UNCHAINED)

Wileton, Knut

Sam leaped into this member of the Tau Kappa Beta fraternity at Meeks College in 1967. The best thing he could find to say about this "troglodyte" was that at least his name wasn't spelled like the lizard. Knut went by the moniker Wild Thing, and his behavior apparently lived up to it. He and his friends did things like use surgical tubing in the chemistry lab as a catapult for water balloons, stuffed cherry bombs down the toilets in the women's dorm, and committed other acts Sam considered rather barbaric. (FRAT)

Wilkins, Annie

A victim of sexual harassment at work who called Dr. Ruth for advice and unknowingly got Sam Beckett. She had just moved to New York, where she was a secretary in a law office. Her boss had taken her out for a welcome drink, but it didn't stop there. Sam prevented the boss from murdering her in retaliation for refusing his advances. She went on to law school and became a pioneer in the field of sexual harassment. (RUTH)

Wilkins, Carl

His wife was being held hostage in the bank by the Walters brothers, and he was upset that the sheriff wasn't doing anything about it. He took advantage of the diversion that Sam used to get out of the bank to get in, and he and John Walters shot each other. Both lived. (LAND)

Wilkins, Cindy

Pregnant bank customer the Walters brothers were holding hostage. Sam convinced her to fake labor in order to create a diversion for him to get out and go check Gus Vernon's records. She was willing to comply because her dad had lost his farm a few years before. (LAND)

Williams, Hubert "Magic", Signalman 2nd Class (US Navy)

Sam leaped into the communications officer of his brother Tom's Bravo Unit on April 7, 1970, just one day before Tom was to die in combat. Magic was the "Radar" of the unit. The first day he arrived, Charlie hit his helicopter with mortar as he was getting off. He alone survived. The next day he tripped a booby trap and survived. Magic seems to have a sixth sense about what's going to happen, and the others in his unit trust him. Apparently Magic is double-jointed, and Sam may have found out exactly how when Maggie Dawson rewarded him for talking Tom into letting her photograph their next mission. After he saved his brother's life, Tom compared him to Sam, who said he had premonitions about the future. Then, as Sam leaped, Tom called him "little brother", his nickname for Sam.

By the way, SEALS never wear underwear, and always leave the top button of their shorts undone. (NAM)

While Sam was at Havenwell, he went straight from Jesse Tyler to Magic. He thought he was in the middle of a Vietcong ambush, so Al told him to just give his name, rank and serial number: Signalman 2nd Class Hubert Williams, D195683. (SHOCK)

Wills, Byron

He was the clients' rep overseeing Carl Granson's fashion shoot with Edie Landsdale. The two clients names were Frank and Irv. (STROBE)

Wills, Dr. Ginny

Professor of Egyptology at Brown University. She and Dr. Dale Conway disappeared in 1957 on a dig for the tomb of Ptah-Hotep. They were swallowed up without a trace. (CURSE)

Wilson, Cameron

Sam leaped into this 17-year-old nerd on June 6, 1961. Upon looking in a mirror, Sam remarked that his kid "loved junk food and had a face to prove it". (CAM)

Wilson, Cheryl

Cameron's 22-year-old sister was engaged to Bob Thompson, a young man well on the way to becoming an alcoholic and abuser just like his father. Bob had promised her that they would go to the south Pacific with the Peace Corps after they got married, but instead had taken a partnership in his father's car dealership. In the original history, she ends up a miserable, battered woman. After Sam proved to her what kind of man Bob really was, she went off to the Peace Corps alone and she and the man she eventually married end up working in Africa. (CAM)

Wilson, Kiki

Looking for a way to deal with the pain of an M.I.A. brother, she volunteered at the Veterans' Hospital in San Diego. Bobby had been part of a team that went on patrol and never came back, and he had been missing for nearly two years. His Special Forces unit had been attached to the CIA, so Al couldn't find out a thing. She found herself attracted to Ron Miller, and when she read Ron's/Sam's palm, she told him his lifeline was long enough for two people, and that he was on a mission to help someone close to him. Before Sam leaped, she received a telegram saying her brother was coming home. She and Miller eventually married and had three children. (NOWHERE)

Wind Walker

The name of a pinto pony Joseph Wasakie once owned. (FREEDOM)

Winger, Dr. Frank

Transferred from Edwards AFB to Cape Canaveral to do research in neurology. His top-secret work involved testing helmets on chimps. He started as a flight surgeon in Korea, but changed to neurology because he thought he could help the pilots more. Winger has an MD from Harvard and spent eight years there specializing in neurology. He stopped his tests with chimps after Bobo/Sam saved him from drowning, yet he developed a helmet that's still in use in the late 1990s. (WRONG)

Winters, Julie

Sue Anne's sister. The pair of them worked at Taylor's Diner. (MEMPHIS)

Winters, Sue Anne

At age 19 she wanted to embark upon a singing career, but it seemed best that she marry Frank Bigley, a southern gentleman who would prefer that his wife not pursue such nonsense. Elvis Presley/Sam helped her start her career, almost at the cost of Elvis's fame. She went on to sing at the Opry, but never made it big. Still, Sue Anne was happy, and started one of the first Elvis Presley fan clubs. (MEMPHIS)

Witchcraft in America

Sam found himself reading this book written by the Rev. John T. Immendorf and published in Boston in 1879 when he leaped into Joshua Rey. (BMAN)

Wizards

A group of boys into Demons and Dragons. Kevin Bruckner was hoping to become a full member of this group. (MOTHER)

Wojohowitz, Col.

Donna Elesee's father. He had walked out on the family when she was seven, and Sam reunited them just before he was shipping out to Vietnam. (CROSSED)

Woman's Collective

Located at 3rd and Buchanan, it was the headquarters of Diane St. Cloud. (LIBERATION)

Wookie

The Bruckners' dog. Well, this *was* 1981. (MOTHER)

Wright, Buddy

Sam observed that this sleazebag was a master of manipulation, and he knew it. The silver-tongued man had worked his way up to Vice President of Development at National Motors, but he didn't have a clue as to what the automotive buying public really wanted. His speciality was having affairs with young women and telling them what a monster his alcoholic wife was. In reality, he and his wife had an arrangement, whereby they each had their own private lives. He wasn't about to divorce her and lose the status he gained when he wed her. Gloria Collins had fallen for him hook, line and sinker, and believed Buddy was going to divorce his wife Gayle and marry her. The man was a big-time chauvinist, telling Sam he likes his coffee like his women – hot and sweet. Sam managed to bring Buddy down a few notches in the end, though. (GLORIA)

Wuthering Heights

Dr. Gerald Bryant was attempting to explain Heathcliff's obsession with Catherine when Sam leaped in. (CROSSED)

X

X-2

Bell's experimental supersonic aircraft. Al helped Sam fly it, but was unable to help him land because it was simply too complicated. Sam nudged it to Mach 3 as the fuel was boiling, then bailed out to safety as the plane exploded. (PILOT)

Y

Yeager, Dorothy

The Coventry town gossip brought some candlesticks to Joshua Ray's home for the haunted house on Halloween. She was killed by a bite from Ray's Black Mamba snake. (BMAN)

York, Tommy, Cadet Lt. Cmdr.

A track star at Prescott Naval Academy in 1964, he had defended his former roommate's choice of a sexual preference, and so found himself being persecuted. After Sam leaped into York, Al assumed the young man was gay. Sam never questioned Tommy's preference, instead asking the question, "Does it matter?" (HONOR)

Young, Daniel "Doc"

Tess McGill challenged this Texas panhandle veterinarian to keep up with her for a week, and if he did he could marry her. She chose Doc figuring he couldn't do it. Sam managed to win the bet, but she instead married Wayne, a hand on the Riata ranche. (TESS)

Z

Zanuck, Darryl F.

The famous movie producer was in the audience at the Las Vegas Golden Sand when Parker, MacKay and Fields made their debut. Parker met his wife through Zanuck. (STAND)

Ziggy

Parallel hybrid computer of Sam's design. Originally the computer was called "he", but after Sam leaped home to 1999 it was shown Ziggy had a female voice. Shortly thereafter the pronoun "she" was used almost exclusively.

Ziggy was given an ego, which was a real breakthrough in computer development. Unfortunately, Sam chose to give the computer the ego of Barbra Streisand, which caused a number of problems. During Sam's first leap, Ziggy refused to accept responsibility for not being able to bring Sam back, and cut power to most of the Project, leaving only essential items available. Ziggy's ego won't allow for a change of mind, either. (PILOT)

The computer was also prone to mood swings, and wouldn't project what would happen to Tim Fox for fear of being wrong (PILOT). Once Ziggy crashed and did screwball things like putting an extra zero on everyone's paycheck, then began to spit out data in foreign languages. Al blamed the problems on foreign microchips (CURSE).

When Elvis Presley was in the Waiting Room, Ziggy became star-struck and operated at a diminished capacity. (MEMPHIS)

Ziggy's main control panel is located in a room that leads to the Imaging and Accelerator Chambers. While in the room, anyone can speak directly to the computer. (BACK)

While Al is in the Imaging Chamber, he communicates with Ziggy, Gooshie and others via a handlink. The handlink has undergone a few design changes, most likely to make it hardier. Al tends to abuse it quite a bit, and one handlink died a spectacular death while Al was attempting to retrieve information about Harry Spontini's divorce. (SPONT)

Using the handlink, Ziggy can project images that Sam, and others who can see Sam, and Al can view. The computer projected the trajectory for pool shots for Sam (POOL), and Al used the link to show Teresa Bruckner pictures of dinosaurs (MOTHER). While masquerading as The Ghost of Christmas Future, Al used the link to project images of Blake Tower and news videos of the millionaire's eventual downfall (MIRACLE).

Ziggy can get a mental link on people close to Sam, but has a difficult time with people who have a few synapses missing in the brain. (PIANO)

Al modified Ziggy's sensors to be a sort of metal detector so he could attempt to find a bullet lodged in the wall of a church in 1971, but he required Tearsa Lorrea to be there in order for the computer to center in on her brain waves. This gave Ziggy a clearer sensory base to pull from. (LAST)

Ziggy nearly lost it when Sam leaped into Jimmy

LaMotta for the second time. She went into maximum overload and kept insisting that history was changing and that things had changed for the LaMotta family, even though Sam wasn't doing anything. Dr. Beeks tried to reason with her, but received a shock which sent her halfway across the room. (EVIL)

Sam programmed Ziggy's memory banks for music, loading in all of Elvis Presley's hits and even a rap song (MEMPHIS, SHOCK). Ziggy digested the entire works of Shakespeare in a matter of seconds, explaining that with a one million gigabyte capacity, she was perfectly capable of rubbing her belly, patting her head and doing a trillion floating point operations at once (BACK).

Using Al's handlink, she was able to create a force field using the electric fences at Mallard Prison in order to keep Thames from getting a lock on Alia. (REVENGE)

Ziggy is also the nickname of a miner Sam encountered at Al's Place. His real name is Simo Servanovich, but he got the moniker Ziggy after he was thrown into a steam radiator during a donkey basketball game. He zigged and zagged for the next week. Ziggy has a bit of problem with words, often susbstituting a sound-alike word instead. "Cabbages" instead of "cartridges", or "canal" instead of "channel". To Sam, Ziggy looked exactly like Moe Stein. (MIRROR)

Zimmerman, Shirl

A member of the congregation at the synagogue where Sam was a rabbi. She had seen Burt Glasserman to be "interviewed" for his book after her father died. She'd been married for 17 years to a man named Howard, who didn't understand her grief. Burt, she believed, did. Their "research" for his book got out of hand, though, and she went to her rabbi for advice. (SHALT)

Zoey

Alia's observer. In some ways, she's just like Al. She's a clothes-horse who loves to lech. After she was able to see Sam as himself, she called him a "studly morsel" and "sweet cheeks". Zoey seems to have much more potential for evil than Alia.

Apparently they've been at this for several years. She told Alia, "We clawed our way out of Hell to land simple assignments like home wrecking and adultery. You don't want to live through the horror we lived through before." She told Lothos she taught Alia, "Every nuance. Every twist. Every lie. She was brilliant." Lothos believed sending Alia out was a mistake, and that he always wanted Zoey to carry out his plan. When Sam shot Zoey, Thames screamed that she was dying. After the familiar flash, Meyers returned and he was unhurt. (EVIL, REVENGE, RETURN)

Episode Guide

Quantum Leap
September 13, 1956; September 1968
(PILOT)

"We did it! . . . Did what?" Sam's memory is so full of holes he doesn't know his own name. What he knows for sure is that he isn't Tom Stratton, an Air Force Pilot set to break Mach 3 in an experimental supersonic aircraft. He also knows he can't fly. Dogging his movements is a mysterious man named Al, who no one else can see. Al finally tells Sam that he is "part of a time travel project that went a little ca-ca," and that they are trying to get him home, and the best he can do is to pretend he's Tom Stratton until they can retrieve him. An ex-astronaut, Al helps Sam fly the experimental craft and then Sam finds he has to stop Stratton's wife from delivering her baby prematurely

Next, he lands in a ballpark as a baseball player in his last professional game. All he has to do is hot a pop fly . . . or does he?

269

Star Crossed
June 15, 1972
(CROSSED)

Sam leaps into Dr. Gerald Bryant, a boozed out literature professor at Lawrence College in 1971. He's there to extricate the professor from a shotgun wedding with Jamie Lee, a student with whom he's been having an affair. While on campus, Sam spots Donna Elesee, the woman he nearly married. She walked out on the wedding, Sam recalls, because of a fear of commitment which he traced to her having been abandoned by her father when she was seven.

Deliberately violating his own rules of time travel, Sam works to reunite Donna with her father in the hope that it will affect his own future.

The Right Hand of God
October 24, 1974
(HAND)

As a boxer whose contract has just been acquired by a group of nuns, Sam must get himself into shape to win a championship fight so the nuns can build a new chapel. Complicating matters is a sleazy promoter who expects Kid Cody/Sam to throw the match, and a girlfriend who wants the boxer to retire.

How The Tess Was Won
August 5, 1956
(TESS)

As a Texas panhandle veterinarian, Sam finds he's got more than sick animals on his hands when he's challenged by Tess McGill to outrope, outride, outdrink and generally outdo her. At stake is her hand in marriage and her father's 50,000 acre spread.

Double Identity
November 8, 1965
(DOUBLE)

After leaping into a rather compromising position, Sam finds out he's a Mafia hit man and the young lady is the godfather's girlfriend. Simply calling off the relationship is not an option, as Ziggy needs Sam to be duplicating the events surrounding his leap-in while they attempt to bring him home. If Sam gets caught in the meantime, he'll find himself singing soprano.

The Color of Truth
August 8, 1955
(COLOR)

As the driver for the widow of a former Alabama governor, Sam learns what it is like to be black in the segregationist south when he sits down at a whites-only lunch counter. While dealing with the repercussions from that incident, he must also make sure his employer does not die in an accident.

The Camikazi Kid
June 6, 1961
(CAM)

Leaping into a nerdy boy with a crater-marked face, Sam has to stop the boy's sister from marrying an abusive man.

Play it Again, Seymour
April 14, 1953
(SEYMOUR)

Sam leaps into a hard-boiled detective who could double for Bogart. The only problem is he's holding a gun over the body of his dead partner. Who killed Phil Grimsley?

Was it his sultry widow Allison? The nerdy newsboy Seymour? Perhaps a "dropper" named Clapper? Sam has to find out, or he could be next.

SECOND SEASON

Honeymoon Express
April 27, 1960
(HONEYMOON)

Leaping into a newlywed on his honeymoon, Sam is there to make sure his lovely bride passes her bar exam. Complicating matters is her murderous ex-husband and Al's insistence that Sam change a major historical event. If he doesn't, Project Quantum Leap might lose funding.

Disco Inferno
April 1, 1976
(DISCO)

Disco. Sam would rather die. But as a stunt man on a disaster movie he must keep his brother from losing his life in a failed stunt.

The Americanization of Machiko
August 4, 1953
(MACHIKO)

Returning from Japan with a surprise war bride, Sam has to convince his family to accept her. Complicating matters are a jealous ex-girlfriend and a prejudiced war veteran.

What Price Gloria?
October 16, 1961
(GLORIA)

Sam leaps into a gorgeous woman and finds out how hard life can be for the other half. Not only does he have to keep his roommate from killing herself over "Mr. Wrong", but Sam has to fend off the sexual advances of his boss, who just happens to be the same man. To make matters worse, Al thinks he's fallen in love with his best friend.

Blind Faith
February 6, 1964
(BLIND)

While leading the life of a blind concert pianist, Sam has to keep his assistant from becoming the next victim of a serial killer.

Good Morning, Peoria
September 9, 1959
(PEORIA)

As a disk jockey at a rock and roll radio station, Sam helps keep the station intact in the face of an attack by self-styled "moralists" in the town. In the meantime, he falls for the station owner.

Thou Shalt Not
February 2, 1974
(SHALT)

Sam leaps into a rabbi and finds his brother's family falling after the death of their son a year earlier. He must patch up the family before his sister-in-law has an affair.

Jimmy
October 14, 1964
(JIMMY)

As a mentally retarded man, Sam learns about a different kind of pejudice while attempting to mainstream the man into society.

273

So Help Me God
July 29, 1957
(HELP)

Defending a black woman against a trumped-up charge of murder puts Sam against an entire Louisiana town. The whites, especially the woman's powerful employer, want her convicted, and the blacks know the truth but refuse to testify.

Catch a Falling Star
May 21, 1979
(CATCH)

Sam does a star turn when he lands as the understudy to the lead in *The Man of La Mancha*. He has to literally keep the drunken star from breaking a leg, but matters become complicated when he meets his old piano teacher. She doesn't know he's Sam Beckett, but he has fallen in love all over again.

A Portrait for Troian
February 7, 1971
(TROIAN)

A beautiful woman believes her dead husband is calling for her to join him, and Sam, as a parapsychologist, has to find the source of the mysterious messages and goings-on.

Animal Frat
October 19, 1967
(FRAT)

Sam has to prevent a fellow college student from dying in a bomb blast set up to protest the war in Vietnam.

Another Mother
September 30, 1981
(MOTHER)

As a divorced mother of three, Sam learns how to juggle fighting kids, burned dinners and a kidnapping. The son will vanish without a trace that night.

All-Americans
November 6, 1962
(ALL)

Leaping into a star high school quarterback, Sam's job is to prevent a teammate from throwing the championship game and blowing a medical school scholarship to protect his illegal – alien mother.

Her Charm
September 6, 1973
(CHARM)

As an FBI agent protecting a witness from the mob, Sam finds that no matter what he does, he cannot seem to prevent her death.

Freedom
November 22, 1970
(FREEDOM)

A young Shoshone Indian is trying to help his grandfather go home to die as Sam leaps into his life. During the journey, Sam faces a painful decision about whether he should prolong the man's life or take him home to die.

Good Night, Dear Heart
November 9, 1957
(DEAR)

After the apparent suicide of a young German immigrant in a seaside resort town, Sam leaps into the town coroner and discovers her death was a murder. Searching for the killer is difficult as Sam finds resistance among the towns-people, who would rather close the book on the incident.

Pool Hall Blues
September 4, 1954
(POOL)

A retired billiards legend shouldn't have to do anything but play pool, and snooker a few unsuspecting opponents for laughs, but the stakes rise after Sam leaps in. The marker is about to be called in on his granddaughter's blues club, and Sam has to play for the marker. Only one minor problem: Sam doesn't know how to play pool.

Leaping in Without a Net
November 18, 1958
(NET)

As a high-flying trapeze artist, Sam has to catch his sister in the dangerous triple somersault. Opposing his efforts is the duo's father, who refuses to let Sam fly because the man he leaped into was catching when their mother died a year before.

Maybe Baby
March 11, 1963
(MAYBE)

On the 1am with a stripper and a kidnapped baby, Sam must decide if the woman is telling the truth about taking the child back to her real mother. In pursuit is the father, who claims to be a widower, and the law.

Sea Bride
June 3, 1954
(BRIDE)

Sam must prevent a wedding on the high seas before the bride marries a Mafia man intent on buying out the shipping business her family owns. His job is complicated by his identity as the bride's ex-husband, who had vanished on a sea voyage and been given up for dead.

M.I.A.
April 1, 1969
(MIA)

When Sam leaps into the life of a San Diego police officer in 1969, Al attempts to convince him that he's there to keep a woman from marrying another man and leaving her M.I.A. husband for dead.

THIRD SEASON

The Leap Home
November 25, 1969
(HOME)

Back home in Elk Ridge, Indiana as himself at age sixteen, Sam has to win a big basketball game so some of his old classmates can go on to college. Instead, he tries to change his own past.

The Leap Home, Pt. II: Vietnam
April 7, 1970
(NAM)

Leaping straight from Elk Ridge to Vietnam, Sam finds himself in his brother Tom's S.E.A.L. unit the day before his death. He can save his brother, but at a terrible price.

Leap of Faith
August 19, 1963
(FAITH)

As a Catholic priest, Sam has to keep a fellow priest, who claimed to have been witness to a murder from becoming a victim himself. Along the way, Sam helps the elder man regain his lost faith.

One Strobe Over the Line
June 15, 1965
(STROBE)

The life of a high-fashion photographer isn't as flashy as it looks, Sam realizes when he has to help a young model whose agent has her hooked on drugs.

The Boogieman
October 31, 1964
(M+BMAN)

As if being a horror novelist on Halloween isn't creepy enough, Sam finds himself powerless to prevent a string of murders. Al thinks the writer's girlfriend is a witch and must be responsible, but there's more to this scary night than meets Sam's eye.

Miss Deep South
June 7, 1958
(SOUTH)

Sam finds himself sash-deep in trouble when he lands in a beauty contestant. While helping keep a fellow-contestant out of the clutches of a sleazy photographer, he must do well in the pageant so the lady he leaped into can afford to go to medical school.

Black and White on Fire
August 11, 1965
(B&W)

In the midst of the Watts Riots, Sam finds himself as a black medical student in love with a white woman.

The Great Spontini
November 9, 1974
(SPONT)

As a blundering magician involved in a bitter custody battle, Sam works to reunite a broken family.

Rebel Without a Clue
September 1, 1958
(REBEL)

Riding with a motorcycle gang, Sam attempts to save a woman from being killed by their Brando-esque leader.

A Little Miracle
December 24, 1962
(MIRACLE)

Sam works to keep a bitter millionaire from evicting a street mission during the holiday season in order to build a towering Manhattan landmark to himself. The only way Sam (as the man's valet) and Al find to possibly turn the man around is to "Scrooge" him on Christmas Eve.

Runaway
July 4, 1964
(RUNAWAY)

Bringing back memories of his own family vacations, Sam finds himself as a kid on a cross-country trip. In between torments from big sister, he has to make sure the mother doesn't run away from the family.

8½ Months
November 15, 1955
(8½)

Sam leaps into the life of a 16-year-old on the verge of giving birth to a baby. While he struggles with all of the attendant feelings of impending motherhood, he has to make sure the girl's baby will have a home rather than be given up for adoption – or he may become the first man in history to have a baby.

Future Boy
October 6, 1957
(FUTURE)

Real life fantasy as Sam lands in the role of an actor in a children's television series about time travel. Unfortunately for the man who plays Captain Galaxy, his own dreams of time travel might land him in the mental institution, and Sam must prevent him from wasting away his life.

Private Dancer
October 6, 1979
(DANCER)

As a Chippendale dancer, Sam fights off adoring fans and works to help a deaf lady achieve her dream of becoming a dancer.

Piano Man
November 10, 1985
(PIANO)

Sam leaps into a lounge lizard who went into hiding after witnessing a Mafia murder. When the musician's old girlfriend tracks him down to convince herself she no longer loves him, they wind up dodging bullets from an unseen assassin who dogs their every move.

Southern Comfort
August 4, 1961
(COMFORTS)

Things get a little uncomfortable for Sam as he becomes the proprietor of a "house of joy" in New Orleans. One of the ladies seems clearly out of place, and Al informs Sam she will vanish unless Sam finds a way to keep her on the premises.

Glitter Rock
April 12, 1974
(ROCK)

As the leader of a 1970s KISS-like rock group, Sam has to catch a murderer – before he becomes the victim.

A Hunting We Will Go
June 18, 1976
(HUNT)

Sam becomes a bounty hunter leading a feisty woman back to justice – or her death. Is she telling the truth about the crime, or is it another in a long series of escape attempts?

Last Dance Before an Execution
May 12, 1971
(LAST)

In one of his most harrowing leaps ever, Sam arrives just as he is being strapped into the electric chair to due for a murder the man may not have committed. Taking advantage of a last-minute reprieve, he works to find the truth buried in a mass of legal and political red tape.

Heart of a Champion
July 23, 1955
(CHAMP)

Tagging in as one-half of a "bad guy" team of wrestlers, Sam takes a few unplanned knocks when he attempts to keep his partner (and brother) from fighting in the championship match. If he wrestles, he'll die in the ring of heart failure.

Nuclear Family
October 26, 1962
(NUCLEAR)

Amid the backdrop of the Cuban Missile Crisis, Sam finds himself selling fallout shelters in Florida. In two days a neighbor will get killed during a false air-raid alarm, and the salesman's brother will get convicted unless Sam can prevent the death.

Shock Theatre
October 3, 1954
(SHOCK)

When Sam receives a high does of shock therapy in a mental institution, he begins to exhibit personalities from past leaps. With each change, Al finds it harder to contact Sam. Unless Sam can snap back to reality, contact may be lost forever.

FOURTH SEASON

The Leap Back
June 15, 1945, September 18, 1999
(BACK)

A well-timed lightning bolt at the end of his previous leap caused Al and Sam to switch places, with Sam as the hologram and Al in 1945, as a POW just home from the Second World War. While the past comes flooding back to Sam, Al has to prevent a lover's leap to death.

Play Ball
August 6, 1961
(BALL)

Sam finds himself back on the baseball diamond, this time as a former major league pitcher stuck back in the minors. While fighting off the advances of the team's owner and her daughter, Sam has to help a hot rookie pitcher overcome his drinking and self-loathing.

Hurricane
August 17, 1969
(HURRICANE)

While Hurricane Camille is pounding the Gulf coast, Sam seems to be faced with a terrible choice. Does he save the hurricane-watching party the deputy he leaped into did originally, or save the man's girlfriend? Of course, Sam attempts to do both.

Justice
May 11, 1955
(JUSTICE)

Sam is disgusted to find himself being inducted into the Ku Klux Klan, a group which stands for everything his parents taught him to fight against. While following the rules which say he has to act like the person he's leaped into, Sam has to prevent the lynching of a local black activist.

Permanent Wave
June 2, 1983
(PERM)

Sam leaps into *the* hairdresser in Beverly Hills in time for his girlfriend's son to witness a robbery/murder at the pharmacy next door. She refuses to let her son speak to the police, and they begin to be dogged by a killer intent on silencing the boy forever.

Raped
June 20, 1980
(RAPED)

No one wants to believe a teenage rape victim, Sam learns, especially when the accused is the son of prominent people. As the victim, Sam attempts to make the charges stick.

The Wrong Stuff
January 24, 1961
(WRONG)

In a genetic twist on leaping, Sam finds himself in the chimponaut corps – as one of the space cadets. His mission is to get himself into the space program or the chimp will disappear.

Dreams
February 28, 1979
(DREAMS)

After leaping into the life of a homicide detective investigating a gruesome murder, he begins to have strange flashbacks. After visiting the psychiatrist who had been treating the murdered woman, Sam is drawn into a deadly quest for the source of the visions.

A Single Drop of Rain
September 7, 1953
(RAIN)

Sam becomes a traveling rain maker who has just returned to his drought-stricken hometown. His brother thinks he's a huckster, but his sister-in-law is ready to run away with him. Sam works to reunite the family and to make it rain despite the odds.

Unchained
November 2, 1956
(UNCHAINED)

Working on a chain gang in Louisiana, Sam has to help his "shackle mate" who has been unjustly accused of robbery.

The Play's the Thing
September 9, 1969
(PLAY)

As the much younger half of a May-December romance, Sam must convince the woman he's living with not to consign herself to a fate worse than death: moving back to Cleveland with her "square" son and his wife. In the meantime, he has to go on-stage as Hamlet – in the nude.

Running for Honor
June 11, 1964
(HONOR)

Al becomes very upset when Sam leaps into a track student at a Naval academy who is defending his ex-roommate's homosexuality. While Sam works to convince his friend that perhaps the military hard anti-gay line is wrong, he has to keep the man's friend from being murdered by a gay-bashing gang.

Temptation Eyes
February 1, 1985
(EYES)

Sam leaps into a television reporter investigating a string of murders in San Francisco, and has to keep a psychic helping the police from becoming the next victim. The stake becomes more personal after she discovers his identity and the pair have an intense love affair.

The Last Gunfighter
November 28, 1957
(GUN)

As an old gunfighter who now makes his living by re-enacting his supposed fight to clean up an Arizona town, Sam is confronted by the man's ex-partner who claims *he* was the real hero. Sam, works to find a way out of the impending showdown at high noon and to keep the respect of the old man's grandson.

A Song for the Soul
April 7, 1963
(SONG)

Leaping into one-third of a Supremes-style teenage singing group, Sam has to convince one of the other singers not to enter into a recording contract with a sleazy promoter.

Ghost Ship
August 13, 1956
(SHIP)

Once again Sam finds himself in the cockpit (and still unable to fly) co-piloting a corporate jet taking a honeymooning couple to Bermuda. While crossing the Bermuda Triangle, the new wife suffers from a ruptured appendix, and the pilot begins to have flashbacks from an old mission during the war.

Roberto!
July 27, 1982
(ROBERTO)

Sam leaps into a Geraldo-type television reporter who is challenged by a co-worker to do one decent investigative story. The pair uncover a secret chemical weapons plant, and face a corporation eager to do anything – including murder – to keep their secret under wraps.

It's a Wonderful Leap
May 10, 1958
(WONDERFUL)

While working as a cab driver attempting to earn his own medallion in a contest, Sam encounters a woman who claims to be an angel.

Moments to Live
May 4, 1985
(MOMENTS)

In a twist on *Misery*, Sam becomes a soap opera star who is kidnapped by an obsessed fan who wants him to father her child.

The Curse of Ptah-Hotep
March 2, 1957
(CURSE)

Sam lives out a childhood dream when he leaps into an archaeologist about to break into the fabled tomb of the pharaoh Ptah-Hotep. Legends about a curse seem to come true as their encampment is plagued with a number of accidents, including an impending sandstorm that will obscure the site of the tomb forever.

Stand Up
April 30, 1959
(STAND)

Leaping into the nightclub circuit, Sam finds himself part of a comedy act. His male partner is consumed with anger and he is in love with the female partner, but they can't seem to get together. While Sam works to bring them together, he must stop a Mafia-connected hotel owner who has designs on the woman.

A Leap for Lisa
June 25, 1957
(LISA)

Sam has a chance to change Al's history when he leaps into his best friend in 1957. Al is facing a charge of murdering his commanding officer's wife, and his alibi is that he was with Lisa Sherman, a married nurse. Sam told Lisa not to testify, and she died in a car wreck that evening. In the original history Lisa told Al's lawyer they were, which got Al off the hook. Now Sam is faced with proving Al's innocence as the odds of his court martial and subsequent execution rise.

FIFTH SEASON

Lee Harvey Oswald
March 21, 1963; October 5-6, 1957; June 6, 1959; October 21,
1959; April 10, 1963; October 21, 1963; November 22, 1963
(LHO)

Sam's first leap into a historical figure finds him as Lee
Harvey Oswald, the man accused of assassinating John F.
Kennedy. During a series of leaps through Oswald's adult
life, the two minds become entangled to the point that
Sam finds himself in the Texas Schoolbook Depository
with his finger on the trigger.

Leaping of the Shrew
September 27, 1956
(SHREW)

Shipwrecked with a spoiled heiress, Sam has to help her
follow her heart and marry the Greek seaman he leaped
into.

Nowhere to Run
August 10, 1968
(NOWHERE)

As a soldier who lost his legs in Vietnam, Sam struggles to
hold together a marriage and keep his hospital roommate
from killing himself.

Killin' Time
June 18, 1958
(KILLIN)

Sam leaps into a serial killer holding a woman and her
daughter hostage. Back in the Waiting Room, the killer
escapes and Al has to track him down before Sam can leap.

Otherwise, Sam will die when the sheriff storms the house.

Star Light, Star Bright
May 21, 1966
(BRIGHT)

When Sam witnesses a UFO, he has to convince the family he lives with that the old man he has leaped into is telling the truth before he gets committed to a mental institution.

Deliver Us From Evil
March 12, 1966
(EVIL)

Sam is delighted to be back as Jimmy, the man with Down's Syndrome he had mainstreamed on an earlier leap. While things look great on the surface, underneath the family is falling apart. The cause becomes evident when he touches Connie and suddenly sees her as Alia, another time traveler. Her project has a less-than-decent intent, as Sam finds out to his horror.

One Little Heart
August 8, 1955
For Your Love
June 14, 1966
The Last Door
July 19, 1978
(TRILOGY)

In a triple leap, Sam finds himself drawn to a young woman accused or murdering one of her friends and then the friend's father. Abagail's accuser is the one survivor of the family, and believes the child is cursed. Leta's insistent accusations drive her to set Abagail's house on fire, and Sam rescues her, leaping moments before Abagail's father died in the fire.

Sam next finds himself as Abagail's fiancé, and is strongly attracted to her himself. Again, she is accused of a murder when a child she was baby-sitting runs away. Sam convinces a lynch mob instigated by Leta not to hang her.

The old murder charges surface in 1978, when Sam leaps into a lawyer defending Abagail for the murder of Leta. Other surprises are in store when Sam discovers Abagail has a child conceived during his last leap.

Promised Land
December 22, 1971
(LAND)

Once again in his hometown of Elk Ridge, Sam is one of three brothers robbing the bank in desperation to pay off their loan. Sounds crazy, but half of the townspeople support them because their farms are in trouble. Sam digs to find the reason the bank lent farmers money they couldn't pay back while attempting to keep violence from erupting at the bank.

A Tale of Two Sweeties
February 25, 1958
(TALE)

Sam finds himself between a rock and a hard place when he leaps into a bigamist. Ziggy says he has to choose one of two wives and keep each from finding out about the other.

Liberation
October 16, 1968
(LIBERATION)

As a middle-aged housewife turned bra-burning liberationist, Sam must keep the woman's husband from walking out on the family and their daughter from dying in an ill-advised protest march that turns violent.

Dr. Ruth
April 25, 1985
(RUTH)

For his second leap into a famous person, Sam becomes the sex therapist Dr. Ruth Westheimer and has lots of trouble dealing with the frank language shared during her radio program. His job is twofold: to get his producer's and announcer's on-again, off-again relationship permanently on; and to help a woman who is being sexually harassed on the job. In the future, Al takes a little advice from the real Dr. Ruth.

Blood Moon
March 10, 1975
(BLOOD)

Sam leaps into the coffin of an artist who lives as a vampire – on the night of the sacrifice to Count Bathory. Sam believes the man is just very eccentric, but Al thinks otherwise. Matters are complicated by a couple who arrive to share the ritual, and Sam must save the artist's girlfriend from being the sacrifice.

Evil Leaper II: Return
October 8, 1956
(RETURN)

Once again, Sam meets up with Alia, the time traveler with less-than-good intentions. The pair are on a college campus, and her intent is to stop the goody-two-shoes hijinks of the student Sam has leaped into. Alia has begun to feel trapped, forced into her deeds by her observer, Zoey, and Lothos, the computer behind her project. Sam and Alia plan a desperate escape to free Alia.

Evil Leaper II: Revenge
September 16, 1987
(REVENGE)

Sam and Alia leap together, into a woman's prison where they are accused of murdering another inmate. Zoey leaps into the fray as the prison warden, and Sam and Al work to mask Alia from Zoey and Lothos.

Goodbye, Norma Jean
April 4, 1960
(NORMA)

As Marilyn Monroe's driver, Sam must keep the star alive to make one last movie.

The Beast Within
November 6, 1972
(BEAST)

Leaping into a Vietnam vet living as a mountain man, Sam is startled when a boy mistakes him dressed in a furry coat for the legendary monster Bigfoot. The vet lives with a friend who is suffering seizures and hallucinations related to a war injury, and his attempts to get medicine are foiled by the sheriff, who served with them and has a terrible secret to keep.

The Leap Between the States
September 20, 1862
(STATES)

All the rules are broken when Sam leaps along his genetic code into his own great-grandfather during the Civil War. Sam has to help the Underground Railroad conduct one more family, plus keep the relationship with his future great-grandfather going.

Memphis Melody
July 3, 1954
(MEMPHIS)

Once again Sam leaps into a famous person. This time he's Elvis Presley, but it's two days before The King gets discovered. Sam's task is to help a young woman pursue a singing career while keeping Elvis's career from going down the toilet.

Mirror Image
August 8, 1953
(MIRROR)

Sam walks into a bar the day he is born and sees his own reflection in the mirror. Back at the Project there is no body, and Al and Gooshie set out to find Sam. Meanwhile, Sam is learning a thing or two about the "unknown force" that is directing his leaps, and gets a chance to set right a major wrong in Al's life.